THE WHO'S BUYING SERIES
BY THE NEW STRATEGIST EDITORS

Who's Buying

for Pets

11th EDITION

New Strategist Press, LLC.
P.O. Box 635, Amityville, New York 11701
800/848-0842; 631-608-8795
www.newstrategist.com

© 2014. NEW STRATEGIST PRESS, LLC.

ISBN 978-1-940308-59-3 (paper)
ISBN 978-1-940308-60-9 (e-book)

Printed in the United States of America.

Contents

Household Spending on Pets by Product Category, 2012

About the Data in *Who's Buying for Pets*

Introduction

The spending data in *Who's Buying for Pets* are based on the Bureau of Labor Statistics' Consumer Expenditure Survey, an ongoing, nationwide survey of household spending. The Consumer Expenditure Survey is a complete accounting of household expenditures. It includes everything from big-ticket items, such as homes and cars, to small purchases like laundry detergent and videos. The survey does not include expenditures by government, business, or institutions. The data in this report are from the 2012 Consumer Expenditure Survey, unless otherwise noted.

To produce this report, New Strategist Press analyzed the Consumer Expenditure Survey's average household spending data in a variety of ways, calculating household spending indexes, aggregate (or total) household spending, and market shares. This report shows spending data by age, household income, household type, race, Hispanic origin, region of residence, and education. These analyses are presented in two formats—for all product categories by demographic characteristic and for all demographic characteristics by product category.

Definition of Consumer Unit

The Consumer Expenditure Survey uses the consumer unit rather than the household as the sampling unit. The term "household" is used interchangeably with the term "consumer unit" in this report for convenience, although they are not exactly the same. Some households contain more than one consumer unit.

The Bureau of Labor Statistics defines consumer units as either: (1) members of a household who are related by blood, marriage, adoption, or other legal arrangements; (2) a person living alone or sharing a household with others or living as a roomer in a private home or lodging house or in permanent living quarters in a hotel or motel, but who is financially independent; or (3) two or more persons living together who pool their income to make joint expenditure decisions. The bureau defines financial independence in terms of "the three major expense categories: housing, food, and other living expenses. To be considered financially independent, at least two of the three major expense categories have to be provided by the respondent."

The Census Bureau uses the household as its sampling unit in the decennial census and in the monthly Current Population Survey. The Census Bureau's household "consists of all persons who occupy a housing unit. A house, an apartment or other groups of rooms, or a single room is regarded as a housing unit when it is occupied or intended for occupancy as separate living quarters; that is, when the occupants do not live and eat with any other persons in the structure and there is direct access from the outside or through a common hall."

The definition goes on to specify that "a household includes the related family members and all the unrelated persons, if any, such as lodgers, foster children, wards, or employees who share the housing unit. A person living alone in a housing unit or a group of unrelated persons sharing a housing unit as partners is also counted as a household. The count of households excludes group quarters."

Because there can be more than one consumer unit in a household, consumer units outnumber households by several million. Young adults under age 25 head most of the additional consumer units.

How to Use the Tables in This Report

The starting point for all calculations are the unpublished, detailed average household spending data collected by the Consumer Expenditure Survey. These numbers are shown on the report's average spending tables and on each of the product-specific tables. New Strategist's editors calculated the other figures in the report based on the average figures. The indexed spending tables and the indexed spending column (Best Customers) on the product-specific tables reveal whether spending by households in a given segment is above or below the average for all households and by how much. The total (or aggregate) spending tables show the overall size of the market. The market share tables and market share column (Biggest Customers) on the product-specific tables reveal how much spending each household segment controls. These analyses are described in detail below.

• **Average Spending.** The average spending figures show the average annual spending of households on pets in 2012. The Consumer Expenditure Survey produces average spending data for all households in a segment, e.g., all households with a householder aged 25 to 34, not just for those who purchased an item. When examining spending data, it is important to remember that by including both purchasers and nonpurchasers in the calculation, the average is less than the amount spent on the item by buyers. (See Table 1 for the percentage of households that spent on pets in 2012 and how much the purchasers spent.)

Because average spending figures include both buyers and nonbuyers, they reveal spending patterns by demographic characteristic. By knowing who is most likely to spend on an item, marketers can target their advertising and promotions more efficiently, and businesses can determine the market potential of a product or service in a city or neighborhood. By multiplying the average amount households spend on veterinary services by the number of households in an area, for example, the owners of a veterinary clinic can determine where to site their business.

• **Indexed Spending (Best Customers).** The indexed spending figures compare the spending of each household segment with that of the average household. To compute the indexes, New Strategist divides the average amount each household segment spends on an item by average household spending and multiplies the resulting figure by 100.

An index of 100 is the average for all households. An index of 125 means the spending of a household segment is 25 percent above average (100 plus 25). An index of 75 indicates spending that is 25 percent below the average for all households (100 minus 25). Indexed spending figures identify the best customers for a product or service. Households with an index of 178 for pet food, for example, are a strong market for this product. Those with an index below 100 are a weak market.

Spending indexes can reveal hidden markets—household segments with a high propensity to buy a particular product or service but which are overshadowed by household segments that account for a larger share of the market. Householders aged 65 to 74, for example, account for 16.3 percent of the veterinary services market, just a bit smaller than the 16.5 percent accounted for by householders aged 35 to 44. But a look at the indexed spending figures reveals older householders to be the better customers. Householders aged 65 to 74 spend 35 percent more than the average household on veterinary care (index of 135) compared with slightly below-average spending by householders aged 35 to 44 (index of 95). Veterinarians can use this information to target their best customers.

Note that because of sampling errors, small differences in index values may be insignificant. But the broader patterns revealed by indexes can guide marketers to the best customers.

• **Market Shares (Biggest Customers).** New Strategist produces market share figures by converting total (aggregate) spending data into percentages. To calculate the percentage of total spending on an item that is controlled by each demographic segment—i.e., its market share—each segment's total spending on an item is divided by aggregate household spending on the item.

Market shares reveal the biggest customers—the demographic segments that account for the largest share of spending on a particular product or service. In 2012, for example, households headed by people aged 45 to 64 accounted for 57 percent of spending on pet services. By targeting only these consumers, pet service providers could reach the majority of their customers. There is a danger here, however. By single-mindedly targeting the biggest customers, businesses cannot nurture potential growth markets. With competition for customers more heated than ever, targeting potential markets is increasingly important to business survival.

• **Product-Specific Tables.** The product-specific tables reveal at a glance the demographic characteristics of spending by individual product category. These tables show average spending, indexed spending (Best Customers), and market shares (Biggest Customers) by age, income, household type, race and Hispanic origin, region of residence, and education. If you want to see the spending pattern for an individual product at a glance, these are the tables for you.

History and Methodology of the Consumer Expenditure Survey

The Consumer Expenditure Survey is an ongoing study of the day-to-day spending of American households. In taking the survey, government interviewers collect spending data on products and services as well as the amount and sources of household income, changes in saving and debt, and demographic and economic characteristics of household members. The Bureau of the Census collects data for the Consumer Expenditure Survey under contract with the Bureau of Labor Statistics, which is responsible for analysis and release of the survey data.

Since the late 19th century, the federal government has conducted expenditure surveys about every 10 years. Although the results have been used for a variety of purposes, their primary application is to track consumer prices. In 1980, the Consumer Expenditure Survey became continuous with annual release of data. The survey is used to update prices for the market basket of products and services used in calculating the Consumer Price Index.

The Consumer Expenditure Survey consists of two separate surveys: an interview survey and a diary survey. In the interview portion of the survey, respondents are asked each quarter for five consecutive quarters to report their expenditures for the previous three months. The interview survey records purchases of big-ticket items such as houses, cars, and major appliances, and recurring expenses such as insurance premiums, utility payments, and rent. The interview component covers about 95 percent of all expenditures.

The diary survey records expenditures on small, frequently purchased items during a two-week period. These detailed records include expenses for food and beverages purchased in grocery stores and at restaurants, as well as other items such as tobacco, housekeeping supplies, nonprescription drugs, and personal care products and services. The diary survey is intended to capture expenditures respondents are likely to forget or recall incorrectly over longer periods of time.

Two separate, nationally representative samples are used for the interview and diary surveys. For the interview survey, about 7,000 consumer units are interviewed on a rotating panel basis each quarter for five consecutive quarters. Another 7,000 consumer units kept weekly diaries of spending for two consecutive weeks. Data collection is carried out in 91 areas of the country.

The Bureau of Labor Statistics reviews, audits, and cleanses the data, then weights them to reflect the number and characteristics of all U.S. consumer units. Like any sample survey, the Consumer Expenditure Survey is subject to two major types of error. Nonsampling error occurs when respondents misinterpret questions or interviewers are inconsistent in the way they ask questions or record answers. Respondents may forget items, recall expenses incorrectly, or deliberately give wrong answers. A respondent may remember how much he or she spent at the grocery store but forget the items picked up at a local convenience store. Mistakes during the various stages of data processing and refinement can also cause nonsampling error.

Sampling error occurs when a sample does not accurately represent the population it is supposed to represent. This kind of error is present in every sample-based survey and is minimized by using a proper sampling procedure. Standard error tables documenting the extent of sampling error in the Consumer Expenditure Survey are available from the Bureau of Labor Statistics at http://www .bls.gov/cex/csxcombined.htm.

Although the Consumer Expenditure Survey is the best source of information about the spending behavior of American households, it should be treated with caution because of the above problems.

For More Information

To find out more about the Consumer Expenditure Survey, contact the specialists at the Bureau of Labor Statistics at (202) 691-6900, or visit the Consumer Expenditure Survey home page at http://www.bls.gov/cex/. The web site includes news releases, technical documentation, and current and historical summary-level data. The detailed average spending data shown in this report are available from the Bureau of Labor Statistics only by special request.

For a comprehensive look at detailed household spending data for all products and services, see the 19th edition of *Household Spending: Who Spends How Much on What*. New Strategist's books are available in hardcopy or as downloads with links to the Excel version of each table. Find out more by visiting http://www.newstrategist.com or by calling 1-800-848-0842.

Table 1. Percent reporting expenditure and amount spent, average week or quarter, 2012

(percent of consumer units reporting expenditure and amount spent by purchasers during the average week or quarter, 2012)

	average week	
	percent reporting expenditure	amount spent by purchasers
Pets	**19.8%**	**$40.95**
Pet food	16.7	22.46
Pet purchase, supplies, and medicines	6.0	25.13
Veterinary services	1.7	174.55

	average quarter	
	percent reporting expenditure	amount spent by purchasers
Pets	**29.2%**	**$253.73**
Pet purchase, supplies, and medicines	22.6	150.30
Pet services	6.1	169.79
Veterinary services	10.0	298.47

Note: Households were asked about their spending on "pets," "pet purchase, supplies, and medicines," and "veterinary services" on both the diary survey (weekly amount) and interview survey (quarterly amount).
Source: Calculations by New Strategist based on the Bureau of Labor Statistics' 2012 Consumer Expenditure Survey

Household Spending Trends, 2000 to 2012

Household spending declined during the Great Recession and its aftermath, bottoming out in 2010. Then things began to get better. Between 2010 and 2012, average annual household spending climbed 1.6 percent to $51,442, after adjusting for inflation. The 2012 figure was still 6.7 percent below the 2006 peak, however, when the average household spent $55,119.

Although household spending is growing again, the average household is spending less than it did in 2006 on most items. Spending on alcoholic beverages is an example. Although the average household spent 4 percent more on alcoholic beverages in 2012 ($451) than in 2010 ($434), the 2012 figure is 20 percent below the 2006 figure ($566). Many categories show a similar pattern. The average household spent 5 percent more on furniture in 2012 ($391) than in 2010 ($374), but the amount spent by the average household on furniture in 2012 was 26 percent below the spending of 2006 ($527). Spending on new cars and trucks increased by a substantial 28 percent between 2010 and 2012, but the 2012 figure was still 20 percent below the level of 2006.

Other categories continued their decline in the 2010-to-2012 time period, despite the overall spending recovery. Average household spending on mortgage interest fell 13 percent between 2010 and 2012, after adjusting for inflation, as more Americans chose to rent rather than buy a home. Spending on apparel continued its long-term decline. Conversely, a handful of spending categories have grown steadily despite the Great Recession, including health insurance, medical services, education, and the category "pets, toys, and playground equipment" (dominated by pet spending).

Although household spending is beginning to recover from the Great Recession, the recovery is slow and spending on many categories continues to decline. But those who have been eagerly awaiting good economic news should take heart at the spending boost for items such as new cars and trucks, household textiles, reading material, footwear, personal care products and services, cash contributions, and gifts for people in other households. Americans may be starting to open their wallets, at least a bit.

Households are spending more, but still less than they once did

(percent change in spending by the average household on selected products and services, 2006, 2010, and 2012; in 2012 dollars)

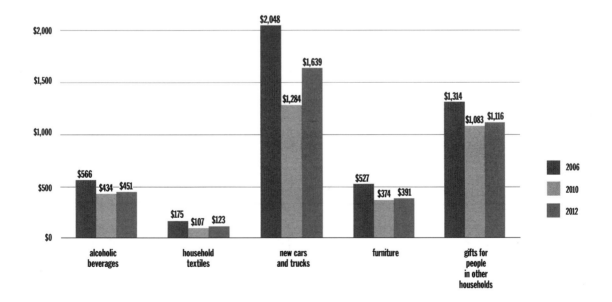

Table 2. Household spending trends, 2000 to 2012

(average annual spending of total consumer units, 2000, 2006, 2010, and 2012; percent change, 2000–06, 2006–12, and 2010–12; in 2012 dollars)

	average annual household spending (in 2012$)				percent change		
	2012	2010	2006	2000	2010–12	2006–12	2000–06
Number of consumer units (in 000s)	124,416	121,107	118,843	109,367	2.7%	4.7%	8.7%
Average annual spending of consumer units	$51,442	$50,655	$55,118	$50,725	1.6	–6.7	8.7
FOOD	**6,599**	**6,453**	**6,960**	**6,877**	**2.3**	**–5.2**	**1.2**
Food at home	**3,921**	**3,816**	**3,891**	**4,028**	**2.8**	**0.8**	**–3.4**
Cereals and bakery products	538	529	508	604	1.8	5.9	–15.9
Cereals and cereal products	182	174	163	208	4.8	11.8	–21.7
Bakery products	356	355	346	396	0.3	2.8	–12.6
Meats, poultry, fish, and eggs	852	825	908	1,060	3.2	–6.1	–14.4
Beef	226	228	269	317	–1.1	–15.9	–15.3
Pork	166	157	179	223	5.8	–7.2	–19.7
Other meats	122	123	120	135	–1.0	2.0	–11.2
Poultry	159	145	161	193	9.4	–1.0	–16.9
Fish and seafood	126	123	139	147	2.3	–9.3	–5.3
Eggs	53	48	42	45	9.4	25.8	–7.0
Dairy products	419	400	419	433	4.7	0.0	–3.3
Fresh milk and cream	152	148	159	175	2.4	–4.7	–8.7
Other dairy products	267	253	260	257	5.7	2.8	0.9
Fruits and vegetables	731	715	674	695	2.2	8.4	–2.9
Fresh fruits	261	244	222	217	6.8	17.5	2.2
Fresh vegetables	226	221	220	212	2.2	2.8	3.7
Processed fruits	114	119	124	153	–4.2	–8.2	–19.0
Processed vegetables	130	131	108	112	–0.4	20.2	–3.4
Other food at home	1,380	1,346	1,380	1,236	2.6	0.0	11.7
Sugar and other sweets	147	139	142	156	5.8	3.3	–8.7
Fats and oils	114	108	98	111	5.1	16.4	–11.5
Miscellaneous foods	699	702	714	583	–0.5	–2.1	22.6
Nonalcoholic beverages	370	351	378	333	5.5	–2.1	13.4
Food prepared by consumer unit on trips	50	45	49	53	10.4	2.1	–8.2
Food away from home	**2,678**	**2,638**	**3,068**	**2,849**	**1.5**	**–12.7**	**7.7**
ALCOHOLIC BEVERAGES	**451**	**434**	**566**	**496**	**4.0**	**–20.3**	**14.1**
HOUSING	**16,887**	**17,433**	**18,639**	**16,425**	**–3.1**	**–9.4**	**13.5**
Shelter	**9,891**	**10,331**	**11,016**	**9,485**	**–4.3**	**–10.2**	**16.1**
Owned dwellings	6,056	6,609	7,421	6,136	–8.4	–18.4	20.9
Mortgage interest and charges	3,067	3,528	4,274	3,519	–13.1	–28.2	21.5
Property taxes	1,836	1,910	1,878	1,519	–3.9	–2.2	23.7
Maintenance, repair, insurance, other expenses	1,153	1,171	1,270	1,100	–1.5	–9.2	15.4
Rented dwellings	3,186	3,053	2,950	2,712	4.3	8.0	8.8
Other lodging	649	669	646	637	–2.9	0.5	1.3
Utilities, fuels, and public services	**3,648**	**3,854**	**3,869**	**3,319**	**–5.3**	**–5.7**	**16.6**
Natural gas	359	463	580	409	–22.5	–38.1	41.6
Electricity	1,388	1,488	1,442	1,215	–6.7	–3.7	18.7
Fuel oil and other fuels	137	147	157	129	–7.1	–12.8	21.5
Telephone services	1,239	1,240	1,238	1,169	–0.1	0.1	5.9
Water and other public services	525	515	452	395	2.0	16.1	14.6
Household services	**1,159**	**1,060**	**1,080**	**912**	**9.3**	**7.4**	**18.4**
Personal services	368	358	448	435	2.8	–17.8	3.0
Other household services	791	702	632	477	12.6	25.1	32.4
Housekeeping supplies	**610**	**644**	**729**	**643**	**–5.3**	**–16.3**	**13.4**
Laundry and cleaning supplies	155	158	172	175	–1.9	–9.9	–1.5
Other household products	319	346	376	301	–7.9	–15.1	24.7
Postage and stationery	136	139	181	168	–2.1	–24.9	7.8
Household furnishings and equipment	**1,580**	**1,545**	**1,945**	**2,065**	**2.3**	**–18.8**	**–5.8**
Household textiles	123	107	175	141	14.5	–29.9	24.1
Furniture	391	374	527	521	4.6	–25.8	1.1
Floor coverings	16	38	55	59	–57.8	–70.7	–6.8
Major appliances	197	220	274	252	–10.5	–28.2	8.9
Small appliances and miscellaneous housewares	98	113	124	116	–13.0	–21.1	7.0
Miscellaneous household equipment	754	692	789	975	9.0	–4.5	–19.0

	average annual household spending (in 2012$)				percent change		
	2012	2010	2006	2000	2010–12	2006–12	2000–06
APPAREL AND RELATED SERVICES	$1,736	$1,790	$2,134	$2,475	–3.0%	–18.7%	–13.8%
Men and boys	408	402	506	587	1.4	–19.3	–13.8
Men, aged 16 or older	320	320	402	459	0.0	–20.4	–12.3
Boys, aged 2 to 15	88	82	104	128	7.1	–15.1	–19.0
Women and girls	688	698	855	967	–1.4	–19.6	–11.5
Women, aged 16 or older	573	592	716	809	–3.2	–20.0	–11.5
Girls, aged 2 to 15	116	106	139	157	9.1	–16.5	–11.7
Children under age 2	63	96	109	109	–34.2	–42.4	0.0
Footwear	347	319	346	457	8.8	0.2	–24.3
Other apparel products and services	230	275	319	355	–16.3	–27.9	–10.1
TRANSPORTATION	8,998	8,083	9,689	9,889	11.3	–7.1	–2.0
Vehicle purchases	3,210	2,725	3,896	4,557	17.8	–17.6	–14.5
Cars and trucks, new	1,639	1,284	2,048	2,140	27.7	–20.0	–4.3
Cars and trucks, used	1,516	1,388	1,786	2,360	9.2	–15.1	–24.3
Gasoline and motor oil	2,756	2,245	2,536	1,721	22.8	8.7	47.3
Other vehicle expenses	2,490	2,594	2,682	3,041	–4.0	–7.2	–11.8
Vehicle finance charges	223	256	339	437	–12.8	–34.3	–22.4
Maintenance and repairs	814	829	784	832	–1.8	3.9	–5.8
Vehicle insurance	1,018	1,063	1,009	1,037	–4.3	0.9	–2.7
Vehicle rentals, leases, licenses, other charges	434	445	549	735	–2.6	–20.9	–25.3
Public transportation	542	519	575	569	4.4	–5.8	1.0
HEALTH CARE	3,556	3,324	3,150	2,755	7.0	12.9	14.4
Health insurance	2,061	1,928	1,668	1,311	6.9	23.5	27.3
Medical services	839	760	763	757	10.4	10.0	0.8
Drugs	515	511	585	555	0.8	–12.0	5.5
Medical supplies	142	125	133	132	13.3	6.6	0.9
ENTERTAINMENT	2,605	2,637	2,706	2,484	–1.2	–3.7	8.9
Fees and admissions	614	612	690	687	0.4	–11.0	0.5
Audio and visual equipment and services	979	1,004	1,032	829	–2.5	–5.1	24.4
Pets, toys, and playground equipment	648	638	469	445	1.6	38.1	5.4
Other entertainment products and services	363	383	514	524	–5.3	–29.3	–2.0
PERSONAL CARE PRODUCTS AND SERVICES	628	613	666	752	2.5	–5.7	–11.4
READING	109	105	133	195	3.5	–18.2	–31.5
EDUCATION	1,207	1,131	1,011	843	6.7	19.4	20.0
TOBACCO PRODUCTS AND SMOKING SUPPLIES	332	381	372	425	–12.9	–10.9	–12.4
MISCELLANEOUS	829	894	963	1,035	–7.3	–14.0	–6.9
CASH CONTRIBUTIONS	1,913	1,719	2,129	1,589	11.3	–10.1	33.9
PERSONAL INSURANCE AND PENSIONS	5,591	5,657	6,002	4,487	–1.2	–6.8	33.8
Life and other personal insurance	353	335	367	532	5.4	–3.7	–31.1
Pensions and Social Security*	5,238	5,321	5,635	3,955	–1.6	–7.0	*
PERSONAL TAXES	2,226	1,863	2,770	4,156	19.5	–19.6	–33.4
Federal income taxes	1,568	1,196	1,949	3,212	31.1	–19.5	–39.3
State and local income taxes	526	508	591	749	3.6	–11.0	–21.1
Other taxes	132	159	230	195	–17.0	–42.6	18.2
GIFTS FOR PEOPLE IN OTHER HOUSEHOLDS	1,116	1,083	1,314	1,444	3.0	–15.1	–9.0

*Recent spending on pensions and Social Security is not comparable with 2000 because of changes in methodology.
Note: Spending by category does not add to total spending because gift spending is also included in the preceding product and service categories and personal taxes are not included in the total.
Source: Bureau of Labor Statistics, 2000, 2006, 2010, and 2012 Consumer Expenditure Surveys, Internet site http://www.bls.gov/cex/; calculations by New Strategist

Household Spending on Pets, 2000 to 2012

Pet spending is climbing sharply. Between 2000 and 2012, average household spending on pets grew 87 percent, after adjusting for inflation. Spending on pet purchases, supplies, and medicines saw the biggest gain, more than doubling between 2000 and 2012 as pet owners devoted much more money to items such as medications for flea, tick, and heartworm prevention.

The average household spent $522 on pets in 2012. This figure is an average for all households, including those without pets. The Bureau of Labor Statistics reports that during the average week of 2012, 16.7 percent of households bought pet food, for example, spending an average of $22.46. During the average quarter of 2012, 29.2 percent of households spent on pets, devoting $253.73 on average to pets during the quarter.

Most spending in the pet category is for pet food (37 percent), followed by veterinary services (29 percent). Pet purchase, supplies, and medicines absorb another 26 percent of the money spent by the average household on pets, while pet services account for the remaining 8 percent.

Table 3. Pet spending, 2000 to 2012

(average annual and percent distribution of household spending on pets by category, 2000 to 2012; percent change in spending, 2000–06, 2006–12, and 2010–12; in 2012 dollars; ranked by amount spent)

	average annual household spending (in 2012$)				percent change		
	2012	2010	2006	2000	2010–12	2006–12	2000–06
Average household spending on pets	**$522.04**	**$505.49**	**$359.88**	**$279.23**	**3.3%**	**45.1%**	**28.9%**
Pet food	194.70	173.94	151.48	114.62	11.9	28.5	32.2
Veterinarian services	149.95	119.53	106.79	88.00	25.5	40.4	21.4
Pet purchase, supplies, and medicines	135.69	171.11	62.88	50.80	–20.7	115.8	23.8
Pet services	41.70	40.93	38.73	25.81	1.9	7.7	50.1

					percentage point change		
PERCENT DISTRIBUTION OF SPENDING					2010–12	2006–12	2000–06
Average household spending on pets	**100.0%**	**100.0%**	**100.0%**	**100.0%**	–	–	–
Pet food	37.3	34.4	42.1	41.0	2.9	-4.8	1.0
Veterinarian services	28.7	23.6	29.7	31.5	5.1	–1.0	–1.8
Pet purchase, supplies, and medicines	26.0	33.8	17.5	18.2	–7.9	8.5	–0.7
Pet services	8.0	8.1	10.8	9.2	–0.1	–2.8	1.5

Note:Percentage point change calculations are based on unrounded figures. "–" means not applicable.
Source: Bureau of Labor Statistics, 2000, 2006, 2010, and 2012 Consumer Expenditure Surveys; calculations by New Strategist

Household Spending on Pets by Demographic Characteristic, 2012

Spending by Age

Householders ranging in age from 45 to 74 spend more than the average household on pets. The biggest spenders by far are householders aged 55 to 64, who spend 42 percent more than average on pets. The age group spends much more than any other on pet food and veterinary services. The 45-to-54 age group spends the most on pet purchase, supplies, and medicines—36 percent more than average.

Spending by Household Income

Spending on pets rises directly with income. Households with incomes of $100,000 or more spend nearly twice the average on pets. They control 47 percent of the market for pet services and 39 percent of the market for veterinary services. Spending on pets is well below average for households with incomes of less than $50,000.

Spending by Household Type

By household type, the biggest spenders on pets are married couples with school-aged children. They spend 49 percent more than average on pets, and they spend more than other household types on the categories of pet food and pet purchase, supplies, and medicine. Although they are just 21 percent of households, married couples without children at home account for 29 percent of pet spending and spend more than other household types on pet services and veterinary services.

Spending by Race and Hispanic Origin

Non-Hispanic whites completely dominate the pet market, spending 21 percent more than average on their pets. Hispanics spend less than one-half as much as the average household on pets. Asians spend less than one-third of the average, and blacks spend only a bit more than one-quarter of the average. The biggest gap in pet spending between non-Hispanic whites and minorities is for veterinary services.

Spending by Region

Spending on pets does not vary much by household's region of residence, ranging from 5 percent more than average in the West to 6 percent less than average in the Northeast. Households in the West are the best customers of pet food (22 percent more than average) and pet services (20 percent more). Southern households spend the most on veterinary services—13 percent more than the average household.

Spending by Education

Households headed by someone with an associate's degree spend the most on pets—45 percent more than the average household. They spend 65 percent more than average on pet food, while households headed by someone with a bachelor's degree spend 7 percent less than average on this item. Spending on pet services (such as dog day care) is highest among the most educated households—those with a householder who has a graduate degree. Spending on veterinary services also peaks among the most educated households.

Table 4. Pets: Average spending by age, 2012

(average annual spending of consumer units on pets, by age of consumer unit reference person, 2012)

	total consumer units	under 25	25 to 34	35 to 44	45 to 54	55 to 64	65 to 74	75+
Number of consumer units (in 000s)	124,416	8,159	20,112	21,598	24,624	22,770	14,993	12,161
Number of persons per consumer unit	2.5	2.0	2.8	3.4	2.7	2.1	1.8	1.5
Average before-tax income of consumer units	$65,596.00	$36,639.00	$58,832.00	$78,169.00	$81,704.00	$77,507.00	$53,521.00	$33,853.00
Average spending of consumer units, total	51,441.87	31,411.08	49,543.74	58,069.31	62,102.54	55,636.31	45,967.87	33,529.54
Pets	522.04	184.85	403.36	513.62	620.38	739.89	564.24	319.09
Pet food	194.70	90.76	145.13	170.82	218.24	312.50	221.08	96.97
Pet purchase, supplies, and medicines	135.69	73.78	124.11	161.02	184.48	154.95	108.26	50.35
Pet services	41.70	8.24	31.70	39.42	62.54	62.97	32.10	14.55
Veterinary services	149.95	12.07	102.42	142.36	155.13	209.47	202.80	157.23

Source: Bureau of Labor Statistics, unpublished tables from the 2012 Consumer Expenditure Survey

Table 5. Pets: Indexed spending by age, 2012

(indexed average annual spending of consumer units on pets, by age of consumer unit reference person, 2012; index definition: an index of 100 is the average for all consumer units; an index of 125 means that spending by consumer units in that group is 25 percent above the average for all consumer units; an index of 75 indicates spending that is 25 percent below the average for all consumer units)

	total consumer units	under 25	25 to 34	35 to 44	45 to 54	55 to 64	65 to 74	75+
Average spending of consumer units, total	**$51,442**	**$31,411**	**$49,544**	**$58,069**	**$62,103**	**$55,636**	**$45,968**	**$33,530**
Average spending of consumer units, index	**100**	**61**	**96**	**113**	**121**	**108**	**89**	**65**
Pets	**100**	**35**	**77**	**98**	**119**	**142**	**108**	**61**
Pet food	100	47	75	88	112	161	114	50
Pet purchase, supplies, and medicines	100	54	91	119	136	114	80	37
Pet services	100	20	76	95	150	151	77	35
Veterinary services	100	8	68	95	103	140	135	105

Source: Calculations by New Strategist based on the Bureau of Labor Statistics' 2012 Consumer Expenditure Survey

Table 6. Pets: Total spending by age, 2012

(total annual spending on pets, by consumer unit age group, 2012; consumer units and dollars in thousands)

	total consumer units	under 25	25 to 34	35 to 44	45 to 54	55 to 64	65 to 74	75+
Number of consumer units	124,416	8,159	20,112	21,598	24,624	22,770	14,993	12,161
Total spending of all consumer units	$6,400,191,698	$256,283,002	$996,423,699	$1,254,180,957	$1,529,212,945	$1,266,838,779	$689,196,275	$407,752,736
Pets	**64,950,129**	**1,508,191**	**8,112,376**	**11,093,165**	**15,276,237**	**16,847,295**	**8,459,650**	**3,880,453**
Pet food	24,223,795	740,511	2,918,855	3,689,370	5,373,942	7,115,625	3,314,652	1,179,252
Pet purchase, supplies, and medicines	16,882,007	601,971	2,496,100	3,477,710	4,542,636	3,528,212	1,623,142	612,306
Pet services	5,188,147	67,230	637,550	851,393	1,539,985	1,433,827	481,275	176,943
Veterinary services	18,656,179	98,479	2,059,871	3,074,691	3,819,921	4,769,632	3,040,580	1,912,074

Note: Numbers may not add to total because of rounding.
Source: Calculations by New Strategist based on the Bureau of Labor Statistics' 2012 Consumer Expenditure Survey

Table 7. Pets: Market shares by age, 2012

(percentage of total annual spending on pets accounted for by consumer unit age groups, 2012)

	total consumer units	under 25	25 to 34	35 to 44	45 to 54	55 to 64	65 to 74	75+
Share of total consumer units	100.0%	6.6%	16.2%	17.4%	19.8%	18.3%	12.1%	9.8%
Share of total before-tax income	100.0	3.7	14.5	20.7	24.7	21.6	9.8	5.0
Share of total spending	100.0	4.0	15.6	19.6	23.9	19.8	10.8	6.4
Pets	100.0	2.3	12.5	17.1	23.5	25.9	13.0	6.0
Pet food	100.0	3.1	12.0	15.2	22.2	29.4	13.7	4.9
Pet purchase, supplies, and medicines	100.0	3.6	14.8	20.6	26.9	20.9	9.6	3.6
Pet services	100.0	1.3	12.3	16.4	29.7	27.6	9.3	3.4
Veterinary services	100.0	0.5	11.0	16.5	20.5	25.6	16.3	10.2

Note: Numbers may not add to total because of rounding.
Source: Calculations by New Strategist based on the Bureau of Labor Statistics' 2012 Consumer Expenditure Survey

Table 8. Pets: Average spending by income, 2012

(average annual spending on pets, by before-tax income of consumer units, 2012)

	total consumer units	under $20,000	$20,000–$39,999	$40,000–$49,999	$50,000–$69,999	$70,000–$79,999	$80,000–$99,999	$100,000 or more
Number of consumer units (in 000s)	124,416	26,177	28,041	11,010	17,972	6,946	10,977	23,293
Number of persons per consumer unit	2.5	1.8	2.2	2.5	2.6	2.8	2.9	3.2
Average before-tax income of consumer units	$65,596.00	$10,445.26	$29,593.01	$44,759.00	$59,283.00	$74,689.00	$88,974.00	$171,910.00
Average spending of consumer units, total	51,441.87	22,404.57	33,454.51	41,567.34	49,981.57	59,984.14	67,417.91	101,422.59
Pets	**522.04**	**207.31**	**413.44**	**338.25**	**519.97**	**653.82**	**711.68**	**969.19**
Pet food	194.70	85.39	148.98	172.68	192.28	273.89	249.11	333.99
Pet purchase, supplies, and medicines	135.69	60.34	99.82	120.97	133.64	167.33	219.65	223.08
Pet services	41.70	11.69	17.66	20.35	40.99	36.13	69.29	103.66
Veterinary services	149.95	49.89	146.99	24.25	153.07	176.46	173.64	308.45

Source: Bureau of Labor Statistics, unpublished tables from the 2012 Consumer Expenditure Survey

Table 9. Pets: Indexed spending by income, 2012

(indexed average annual spending of consumer units on pets, by before-tax income of consumer unit, 2012; index definition: an index of 100 is the average for all consumer units; an index of 125 means that spending by consumer units in that group is 25 percent above the average for all consumer units; an index of 75 indicates spending that is 25 percent below the average for all consumer units)

	total consumer units	under $20,000	$20,000– $39,999	$40,000– $49,999	$50,000– $69,999	$70,000– $79,999	$80,000– $99,999	$100,000 or more
Average spending of consumer units, total	**$51,442**	**$22,405**	**$33,455**	**$41,567**	**$49,982**	**$59,984**	**$67,418**	**$101,423**
Average spending of consumer units, index	**100**	**44**	**65**	**81**	**97**	**117**	**131**	**197**
Pets	**100**	**40**	**79**	**65**	**100**	**125**	**136**	**186**
Pet food	100	44	77	89	99	141	128	172
Pet purchase, supplies, and medicines	100	44	74	89	98	123	162	164
Pet services	100	28	42	49	98	87	166	249
Veterinary services	100	33	98	16	102	118	116	206

Source: Calculations by New Strategist based on the Bureau of Labor Statistics' 2012 Consumer Expenditure Survey

Table 10. Pets: Total spending by income, 2012

(total annual spending on pets, by before-tax income group of consumer units, 2012; consumer units and dollars in thousands)

	total consumer units	under $20,000	$20,000– $39,999	$40,000– $49,999	$50,000– $69,999	$70,000– $79,999	$80,000– $99,999	$100,000 or more
Number of consumer units	124,416	26,177	28,041	11,010	17,972	6,946	10,977	23,293
Total spending of all consumer units	$6,400,191,698	$586,484,559	$938,098,035	$457,656,413	$898,268,776	$416,649,836	$740,046,398	$2,362,436,389
Pets	**64,950,129**	**5,426,696**	**11,593,341**	**3,724,133**	**9,344,901**	**4,541,434**	**7,812,111**	**22,575,343**
Pet food	24,223,795	2,235,155	4,177,564	1,901,207	3,455,656	1,902,440	2,734,480	7,779,629
Pet purchase, supplies, and medicines	16,882,007	1,579,578	2,799,122	1,331,880	2,401,778	1,162,274	2,411,098	5,196,202
Pet services	5,188,147	306,001	495,078	224,054	736,672	250,959	760,596	2,414,552
Veterinary services	18,656,179	1,305,909	4,121,858	266,993	2,750,974	1,225,691	1,906,046	7,184,726

Note: Numbers may not add to total because of rounding.
Source: Calculations by New Strategist based on the Bureau of Labor Statistics' 2012 Consumer Expenditure Survey

Table 11. Pets: Market shares by income, 2012

(percentage of total annual spending on pets accounted for by before-tax income group of consumer units, 2012)

	total consumer units	under $20,000	$20,000–$39,999	$40,000–$49,999	$50,000–$69,999	$70,000–$79,999	$80,000–$99,999	$100,000 or more
Share of total consumer units	**100.0%**	**21.0%**	**22.5%**	**8.8%**	**14.4%**	**5.6%**	**8.8%**	**18.7%**
Share of total before-tax income	**100.0**	**3.4**	**10.2**	**6.0**	**13.1**	**6.4**	**12.0**	**49.1**
Share of total spending	**100.0**	**9.2**	**14.7**	**7.2**	**14.0**	**6.5**	**11.6**	**36.9**
Pets	**100.0**	**8.4**	**17.8**	**5.7**	**14.4**	**7.0**	**12.0**	**34.8**
Pet food	100.0	9.2	17.2	7.8	14.3	7.9	11.3	32.1
Pet purchase, supplies, and medicines	100.0	9.4	16.6	7.9	14.2	6.9	14.3	30.8
Pet services	100.0	5.9	9.5	4.3	14.2	4.8	14.7	46.5
Veterinary services	100.0	7.0	22.1	1.4	14.7	6.6	10.2	38.5

Note: Numbers may not add to total because of rounding.
Source: Calculations by New Strategist based on the Bureau of Labor Statistics' 2012 Consumer Expenditure Survey

Table 12. Pets: Average spending by high-income consumer units, 2012

(average annual spending on pets, by before-tax income of consumer units with high incomes, 2012)

	total consumer units	$100,000 or more	$100,000– $119,999	$120,000– $149,999	$150,000 or more
Number of consumer units (in 000s)	124,416	23,293	7,183	6,947	9,162
Number of persons per consumer unit	2.5	3.2	3.1	3.2	3.2
Average before-tax income of consumer units	$65,596.00	$171,910.00	$108,977.00	$132,318.00	$251,270.00
Average spending of consumer units, total	51,441.87	101,422.59	77,965.87	89,521.33	129,211.07
Pets	**522.04**	**969.19**	**676.82**	**900.72**	**1,273.95**
Pet food	194.70	333.99	253.62	310.96	422.22
Pet purchase, supplies, and medicines	135.69	223.08	202.22	200.94	256.23
Pet services	41.70	103.66	75.71	81.94	142.05
Veterinary services	149.95	308.45	145.28	306.87	453.45

Source: Bureau of Labor Statistics, unpublished tables from the 2012 Consumer Expenditure Survey

Table 13. Pets: Indexed spending by high-income consumer units, 2012

(indexed average annual spending of consumer units with high incomes on pets, by before-tax income of consumer unit, 2012; index definition: an index of 100 is the average for all consumer units; an index of 125 means that spending by consumer units in that group is 25 percent above the average for all consumer units; an index of 75 indicates spending that is 25 percent below the average for all consumer units)

	total consumer units	$100,000 or more	$100,000– $119,999	$120,000– $149,999	$150,000 or more
Average spending of consumer units, total	$51,442	$101,423	$77,966	$89,521	$129,211
Average spending of consumer units, index	100	197	152	174	251
Pets	**100**	**186**	**130**	**173**	**244**
Pet food	100	172	130	160	217
Pet purchase, supplies, and medicines	100	164	149	148	189
Pet services	100	249	182	196	341
Veterinary services	100	206	97	205	302

Source: Calculations by New Strategist based on the Bureau of Labor Statistics' 2012 Consumer Expenditure Survey

Table 14. Pets: Total spending by high-income consumer units, 2012

(total annual spending on pets, by before-tax income group of consumer units with high incomes, 2012; consumer units and dollars in thousands)

	total consumer units	$100,000 or more	$100,000–$119,999	$120,000–$149,999	$150,000 or more
Number of consumer units	124,416	23,293	7,183	6,947	9,162
Total spending of all consumer units	$6,400,191,698	$2,362,436,389	$560,028,844	$621,904,680	$1,183,831,823
Pets	**64,950,129**	**22,575,343**	**4,861,598**	**6,257,302**	**11,671,930**
Pet food	24,223,795	7,779,629	1,821,752	2,160,239	3,868,380
Pet purchase, supplies, and medicines	16,882,007	5,196,202	1,452,546	1,395,930	2,347,579
Pet services	5,188,147	2,414,552	543,825	569,237	1,301,462
Veterinary services	18,656,179	7,184,726	1,043,546	2,131,826	4,154,509

Note: Numbers may not add to total because of rounding.
Source: Calculations by New Strategist based on the Bureau of Labor Statistics' 2012 Consumer Expenditure Survey

Table 15. Pets: Market shares by high-income consumer units, 2012

(percentage of total annual spending on pets accounted for by before-tax income group of consumer units with high incomes, 2012)

	total consumer units	$100,000 or more	$100,000–$119,999	$120,000–$149,999	$150,000 or more
Share of total consumer units	**100.0%**	**18.7%**	**5.8%**	**5.6%**	**7.4%**
Share of total before-tax income	**100.0**	**49.1**	**9.6**	**11.3**	**28.2**
Share of total spending	**100.0**	**36.9**	**8.8**	**9.7**	**18.5**
Pets	**100.0**	**34.8**	**7.5**	**9.6**	**18.0**
Pet food	100.0	32.1	7.5	8.9	16.0
Pet purchase, supplies, and medicines	100.0	30.8	8.6	8.3	13.9
Pet services	100.0	46.5	10.5	11.0	25.1
Veterinary services	100.0	38.5	5.6	11.4	22.3

Note: Numbers may not add to total because of rounding.
Source: Calculations by New Strategist based on the Bureau of Labor Statistics' 2012 Consumer Expenditure Survey

Table 16. Pets: Average spending by household type, 2012

(average annual spending of consumer units on pets, by type of consumer unit, 2012)

	total consumer units	total married couples	married couples, no children	married couples with children				single parent, at least one child under age 18	single person
				total	oldest child under age 6	oldest child aged 6 to 17	oldest child aged 18 or older		
Number of consumer units (in 000s)	124,416	60,428	25,936	29,252	5,676	14,797	8,778	6,524	36,942
Number of persons per consumer unit	2.5	3.2	2.0	3.9	3.5	4.2	3.9	2.9	1.0
Average before-tax income of consumer units	$65,596.00	$90,393.00	$81,717.00	$98,104.00	$85,200.00	$100,698.00	$102,074.00	$34,194.00	$34,102.00
Average spending of consumer units, total	51,441.87	67,310.04	61,284.60	72,814.06	64,103.17	74,658.88	75,286.36	38,667.27	30,715.83
Pets	**522.04**	**702.30**	**723.51**	**690.06**	**456.52**	**775.29**	**694.34**	**279.50**	**316.68**
Pet food	194.70	262.85	269.46	267.39	196.26	303.34	251.76	100.71	124.04
Pet purchase, supplies, and medicines	135.69	169.31	161.47	172.05	117.47	189.29	178.29	107.18	80.99
Pet services	41.70	59.21	69.22	55.05	53.29	60.31	47.31	27.61	26.09
Veterinary services	149.95	210.93	223.36	195.57	89.50	222.35	216.99	44.00	85.56

Source: Bureau of Labor Statistics, unpublished tables from the 2012 Consumer Expenditure Survey

Table 17. Pets: Indexed spending by household type, 2012

(indexed average annual spending of consumer units on pets, by type of consumer unit, 2012; index definition: an index of 100 is the average for all consumer units; an index of 125 means that spending by consumer units in that group is 25 percent above the average for all consumer units; an index of 75 indicates spending that is 25 percent below the average for all consumer units)

	total consumer units	total married couples	married couples, no children	married couples with children				single parent, at least one child under age 18	single person
				total	oldest child under age 6	oldest child aged 6 to 17	oldest child aged 18 or older		
Average spending of consumer units, total	$51,442	$67,310	$61,285	$72,814	$64,103	$74,659	$75,286	$38,667	$30,716
Average spending of consumer units, index	100	131	119	142	125	145	146	75	60
Pets	**100**	**135**	**139**	**132**	**87**	**149**	**133**	**54**	**61**
Pet food	100	135	138	137	101	156	129	52	64
Pet purchase, supplies, and medicines	100	125	119	127	87	140	131	79	60
Pet services	100	142	166	132	128	145	113	66	63
Veterinary services	100	141	149	130	60	148	145	29	57

Source: Calculations by New Strategist based on the Bureau of Labor Statistics' 2012 Consumer Expenditure Survey

Table 18. Pets: Total spending by household type, 2012

(total annual spending on pets, by consumer unit type, 2012; consumer units and dollars in thousands)

	total consumer units	total married couples	married couples, no children	married couples with children				single parent, at least one child under age 18	single person
				total	oldest child under age 6	oldest child aged 6 to 17	oldest child aged 18 or older		
Number of consumer units	124,416	60,428	25,936	29,252	5,676	14,797	8,778	6,524	36,942
Total spending of all consumer units	$6,400,191,698	$4,067,411,097	$1,589,477,386	$2,129,956,883	$363,849,593	$1,104,727,447	$660,863,668	$252,265,269	$1,134,704,192
Pets	**64,950,129**	**42,438,584**	**18,764,955**	**20,185,635**	**2,591,208**	**11,471,966**	**6,094,917**	**1,823,458**	**11,698,793**
Pet food	24,223,795	15,883,500	6,988,715	7,821,692	1,113,972	4,488,522	2,209,949	657,032	4,582,286
Pet purchase, supplies, and medicines	16,882,007	10,231,065	4,187,886	5,032,807	666,760	2,800,924	1,565,030	699,242	2,991,933
Pet services	5,188,147	3,577,942	1,795,290	1,610,323	302,474	892,407	415,287	180,128	963,817
Veterinary services	18,656,179	12,746,078	5,793,065	5,720,814	508,002	3,290,113	1,904,738	287,056	3,160,758

Note: Numbers do not add to total because not all types of consumer units are shown.
Source: Calculations by New Strategist based on the Bureau of Labor Statistics' 2012 Consumer Expenditure Survey

Table 19. Pets: Market shares by household type, 2012

(percentage of total annual spending on pets accounted for by types of consumer units, 2012)

	total consumer units	total married couples	married couples, no children	married couples with children				single parent, at least one child under age 18	single person
				total	oldest child under age 6	oldest child aged 6 to 17	oldest child aged 18 or older		
Share of total consumer units	**100.0%**	**48.6%**	**20.8%**	**23.5%**	**4.6%**	**11.9%**	**7.1%**	**5.2%**	**29.7%**
Share of total before-tax income	**100.0**	**66.9**	**26.0**	**35.2**	**5.9**	**18.3**	**11.0**	**2.7**	**15.4**
Share of total spending	**100.0**	**63.6**	**24.8**	**33.3**	**5.7**	**17.3**	**10.3**	**3.9**	**17.7**
Pets	**100.0**	**65.3**	**28.9**	**31.1**	**4.0**	**17.7**	**9.4**	**2.8**	**18.0**
Pet food	100.0	65.6	28.9	32.3	4.6	18.5	9.1	2.7	18.9
Pet purchase, supplies, and medicines	100.0	60.6	24.8	29.8	3.9	16.6	9.3	4.1	17.7
Pet services	100.0	69.0	34.6	31.0	5.8	17.2	8.0	3.5	18.6
Veterinary services	100.0	68.3	31.1	30.7	2.7	17.6	10.2	1.5	16.9

Note: Market shares by type of consumer unit do not add to total because not all types of consumer units are shown.
Source: Calculations by New Strategist based on the Bureau of Labor Statistics' 2012 Consumer Expenditure Survey

Table 20. Pets: Average spending by race and Hispanic origin, 2012

(average annual spending of consumer units on pets, by race and Hispanic origin of consumer unit reference person, 2012)

	total consumer units	Asian	black	Hispanic	non-Hispanic white and other
Number of consumer units (in 000s)	124,416	5,393	15,637	15,597	93,385
Number of persons per consumer unit	2.5	2.8	2.5	3.3	2.3
Average before-tax income of consumer units	$65,596.00	$86,156.00	$47,119.00	$48,066.00	$71,552.00
Average spending of consumer units, total	51,441.87	61,399.02	38,626.84	42,267.55	55,096.53
Pets	**522.04**	**161.48**	**146.00**	**253.09**	**629.22**
Pet food	194.70	76.44	59.90	116.46	230.12
Pet purchase, supplies, and medicines	135.69	51.84	46.12	82.95	159.29
Pet services	41.70	12.07	9.14	19.48	50.82
Veterinary services	149.95	21.13	30.84	34.20	188.98

Note: "Asian" and "black" include Hispanics and non-Hispanics who identify themselves as being of the respective race alone. "Hispanic" includes people of any race who identify themselves as Hispanic. "Other" includes people who identify themselves as non-Hispanic and as Alaska Native, American Indian, Asian (who are also included in the "Asian" column), Native Hawaiian or other Pacific Islander, as well as non-Hispanics reporting more than one race.
Source: Bureau of Labor Statistics, unpublished tables from the 2012 Consumer Expenditure Survey

Table 21. Pets: Indexed spending by race and Hispanic origin, 2012

(indexed average annual spending of consumer units on pets, by race and Hispanic origin of consumer unit reference person, 2012; index definition: an index of 100 is the average for all consumer units; an index of 125 means that spending by consumer units in that group is 25 percent above the average for all consumer units; an index of 75 indicates spending that is 25 percent below the average for all consumer units)

	total consumer units	Asian	black	Hispanic	non-Hispanic white and other
Average spending of consumer units, total	**$51,442**	**$61,399**	**$38,627**	**$42,268**	**$55,097**
Average spending of consumer units, index	**100**	**119**	**75**	**82**	**107**
Pets	**100**	**31**	**28**	**48**	**121**
Pet food	100	39	31	60	118
Pet purchase, supplies, and medicines	100	38	34	61	117
Pet services	100	29	22	47	122
Veterinary services	100	14	21	23	126

Note: "Asian" and "black" include Hispanics and non-Hispanics who identify themselves as being of the respective race alone. "Hispanic" includes people of any race who identify themselves as Hispanic. "Other" includes people who identify themselves as non-Hispanic and as Alaska Native, American Indian, Asian (who are also included in the "Asian" column), Native Hawaiian or other Pacific Islander, as well as non-Hispanics reporting more than one race.
Source: Calculations by New Strategist based on the Bureau of Labor Statistics' 2012 Consumer Expenditure Survey

Table 22. Pets: Total spending by race and Hispanic origin, 2012

(total annual spending on pets, by consumer unit race and Hispanic origin groups, 2012; consumer units and dollars in thousands)

	total consumer units	Asian	black	Hispanic	non-Hispanic white and other
Number of consumer units	124,416	5,393	15,637	15,597	93,385
Total spending of all consumer units	$6,400,191,698	$331,124,915	$604,007,897	$659,246,977	$5,145,189,454
Pets	**64,950,129**	**870,862**	**2,283,002**	**3,947,445**	**58,759,710**
Pet food	24,223,795	412,241	936,656	1,816,427	21,489,756
Pet purchase, supplies, and medicines	16,882,007	279,573	721,178	1,293,771	14,875,297
Pet services	5,188,147	65,094	142,922	303,830	4,745,826
Veterinary services	18,656,179	113,954	482,245	533,417	17,647,897

Note: "Asian" and "black" include Hispanics and non-Hispanics who identify themselves as being of the respective race alone. "Hispanic" includes people of any race who identify themselves as Hispanic. "Other" includes people who identify themselves as non-Hispanic and as Alaska Native, American Indian, Asian (who are also included in the "Asian" column), Native Hawaiian or other Pacific Islander, as well as non-Hispanics reporting more than one race. Numbers may not add to total because of rounding.
Source: Calculations by New Strategist based on the Bureau of Labor Statistics' 2012 Consumer Expenditure Survey

Table 23. Pets: Market shares by race and Hispanic origin, 2012

(percentage of total annual spending on pets accounted for by consumer unit race and Hispanic origin groups, 2012)

	total consumer units	Asian	black	Hispanic	non-Hispanic white and other
Share of total consumer units	**100.0%**	**4.3%**	**12.6%**	**12.5%**	**75.1%**
Share of total before-tax income	**100.0**	**5.7**	**9.0**	**9.2**	**81.9**
Share of total spending	**100.0**	**5.2**	**9.4**	**10.3**	**80.4**
Pets	**100.0**	**1.3**	**3.5**	**6.1**	**90.5**
Pet food	100.0	1.7	3.9	7.5	88.7
Pet purchase, supplies, and medicines	100.0	1.7	4.3	7.7	88.1
Pet services	100.0	1.3	2.8	5.9	91.5
Veterinary services	100.0	0.6	2.6	2.9	94.6

Note: "Asian" and "black" include Hispanics and non-Hispanics who identify themselves as being of the respective race alone. "Hispanic" includes people of any race who identify themselves as Hispanic. "Other" includes people who identify themselves as non-Hispanic and as Alaska Native, American Indian, Asian (who are also included in the "Asian" column), Native Hawaiian or other Pacific Islander, as well as non-Hispanics reporting more than one race.
Source: Calculations by New Strategist based on the 2012 Consumer Expenditure Survey

Table 24. Pets: Average spending by region, 2012

(average annual spending of consumer units on pets, by region in which consumer unit lives, 2012)

	total consumer units	Northeast	Midwest	South	West
Number of consumer units (in 000s)	124,416	22,459	27,584	46,338	28,035
Number of persons per consumer unit	2.5	2.4	2.4	2.5	2.6
Average before-tax income of consumer units	$65,596.00	$72,036.00	$65,217.00	$60,219.00	$69,700.00
Average spending of consumer units, total	51,441.87	55,883.88	48,602.08	47,756.69	56,782.20
Pets	**522.04**	**491.93**	**518.61**	**522.50**	**549.16**
Pet food	194.70	175.51	202.04	173.54	238.09
Pet purchase, supplies, and medicines	135.69	133.56	137.71	142.20	124.65
Pet services	41.70	40.19	42.29	36.98	50.13
Veterinary services	149.95	142.67	136.58	169.79	136.29

Source: Bureau of Labor Statistics, unpublished tables from the 2012 Consumer Expenditure Survey

Table 25. Pets: Indexed spending by region, 2012

(indexed average annual spending of consumer units on pets, by region in which consumer unit lives, 2012; index definition: an index of 100 is the average for all consumer units; an index of 125 means that spending by consumer units in that group is 25 percent above the average for all consumer units; an index of 75 indicates spending that is 25 percent below the average for all consumer units)

	total consumer units	Northeast	Midwest	South	West
Average spending of consumer units, total	**$51,442**	**$55,884**	**$48,602**	**$47,757**	**$56,782**
Average spending of consumer units, index	**100**	**109**	**94**	**93**	**110**
Pets	**100**	**94**	**99**	**100**	**105**
Pet food	100	90	104	89	122
Pet purchase, supplies, and medicines	100	98	101	105	92
Pet services	100	96	101	89	120
Veterinary services	100	95	91	113	91

Source: Calculations by New Strategist based on the Bureau of Labor Statistics' 2012 Consumer Expenditure Survey

Table 26. Pets: Total spending by region, 2012

(total annual spending on pets, by region in which consumer unit lives, 2012; consumer units and dollars in thousands)

	total consumer units	Northeast	Midwest	South	West
Number of consumer units	124,416	22,459	27,584	46,338	28,035
Total spending of all consumer units	$6,400,191,698	$1,255,096,061	$1,340,639,775	$2,212,949,501	$1,591,888,977
Pets	**64,950,129**	**11,048,256**	**14,305,338**	**24,211,605**	**15,395,701**
Pet food	24,223,795	3,941,779	5,573,071	8,041,497	6,674,853
Pet purchase, supplies, and medicines	16,882,007	2,999,624	3,798,593	6,589,264	3,494,563
Pet services	5,188,147	902,627	1,166,527	1,713,579	1,405,395
Veterinary services	18,656,179	3,204,226	3,767,423	7,867,729	3,820,890

Note: Numbers may not add to total because of rounding.
Source: Calculations by New Strategist based on the Bureau of Labor Statistics' 2012 Consumer Expenditure Survey

Table 27. Pets: Market shares by region, 2012

(percentage of total annual spending on pets accounted for by consumer units by region of residence, 2012)

	total consumer units	Northeast	Midwest	South	West
Share of total consumer units	**100.0%**	**18.1%**	**22.2%**	**37.2%**	**22.5%**
Share of total before-tax income	**100.0**	**19.8**	**22.0**	**34.2**	**23.9**
Share of total spending	**100.0**	**19.6**	**20.9**	**34.6**	**24.9**
Pets	**100.0**	**17.0**	**22.0**	**37.3**	**23.7**
Pet food	100.0	16.3	23.0	33.2	27.6
Pet purchase, supplies, and medicines	100.0	17.8	22.5	39.0	20.7
Pet services	100.0	17.4	22.5	33.0	27.1
Veterinary services	100.0	17.2	20.2	42.2	20.5

Note: Numbers may not add to total because of rounding.
Source: Calculations by New Strategist based on the Bureau of Labor Statistics' 2012 Consumer Expenditure Survey

Table 28. Pets: Average spending by education, 2012

(average annual spending of consumer units on pets, by education of consumer unit reference person, 2012)

	total consumer units	less than high school graduate	high school graduate	some college	associate's degree	bachelor's degree or more total	bachelor's degree	master's, professional, doctorate
Number of consumer units (in 000s)	124,416	16,246	31,022	25,623	12,287	39,238	24,798	14,440
Number of persons per consumer unit	2.5	2.7	2.5	2.4	2.6	2.4	2.4	2.5
Average before-tax income of consumer units	$65,596.00	$33,154.00	$47,221.00	$55,987.00	$66,122.00	$99,667.00	$89,438.00	$117,233.00
Average spending of consumer units, total	51,441.87	31,193.61	39,989.36	46,118.38	52,414.41	71,926.33	66,420.24	81,363.01
Pets	522.04	302.56	427.60	531.45	755.21	601.44	544.69	697.79
Pet food	194.70	157.31	177.68	197.10	321.85	180.52	172.22	194.55
Pet purchase, supplies, and medicines	135.69	101.02	111.29	139.04	165.80	157.72	149.43	171.95
Pet services	41.70	12.54	23.10	39.53	36.85	71.41	63.85	84.39
Veterinary services	149.95	31.69	115.52	155.78	230.71	191.79	159.18	246.90

Source: Bureau of Labor Statistics, unpublished tables from the 2012 Consumer Expenditure Survey

Table 29. Pets: Indexed spending by education, 2012

(indexed average annual spending of consumer units on pets, by education of consumer unit reference person, 2012; index definition: an index of 100 is the average for all consumer units; an index of 125 means that spending by consumer units in that group is 25 percent above the average for all consumer units; an index of 75 indicates spending that is 25 percent below the average for all consumer units)

	total consumer units	less than high school graduate	high school graduate	some college	associate's degree	bachelor's degree or more total	bachelor's degree	master's, professional, doctorate
Average spending of consumer units, total	$51,442	$31,194	$39,989	$46,118	$52,414	$71,926	$66,420	$81,363
Average spending of consumer units, index	100	61	78	90	102	140	129	158
Pets	100	58	82	102	145	115	104	134
Pet food	100	81	91	101	165	93	88	100
Pet purchase, supplies, and medicines	100	74	82	102	122	116	110	127
Pet services	100	30	55	95	88	171	153	202
Veterinary services	100	21	77	104	154	128	106	165

Source: Calculations by New Strategist based on the Bureau of Labor Statistics' 2012 Consumer Expenditure Survey

Table 30. Pets: Total spending by education, 2012

(total annual spending on pets, by education of consumer unit reference person, 2012; consumer units and dollars in thousands)

	total consumer units	less than high school graduate	high school graduate	some college	associate's degree	bachelor's degree or more		
						total	bachelor's degree	master's, professional, doctorate
Number of consumer units	124,416	16,246	31,022	25,623	12,287	39,238	24,798	14,440
Total spending of all consumer units	$6,400,191,698	$506,771,388	$1,240,549,926	$1,181,691,251	$644,015,856	$2,822,245,337	$1,647,089,112	$1,174,881,864
Pets	64,950,129	4,915,390	13,265,007	13,617,343	9,279,265	23,599,303	13,507,223	10,076,088
Pet food	24,223,795	2,555,658	5,511,989	5,050,293	3,954,571	7,083,244	4,270,712	2,809,302
Pet purchase, supplies, and medicines	16,882,007	1,641,171	3,452,438	3,562,622	2,037,185	6,188,617	3,705,565	2,482,958
Pet services	5,188,147	203,725	716,608	1,012,877	452,776	2,801,986	1,583,352	1,218,592
Veterinary services	18,656,179	514,836	3,583,661	3,991,551	2,834,734	7,525,456	3,947,346	3,565,236

Note: Numbers may not add to total because of rounding.
Source: Calculations by New Strategist based on the Bureau of Labor Statistics' 2012 Consumer Expenditure Survey

Table 31. Pets: Market shares by education, 2012

(percentage of total annual spending on pets accounted for by consumer unit educational attainment groups, 2012)

	total consumer units	less than high school graduate	high school graduate	some college	associate's degree	bachelor's degree or more total	bachelor's degree	master's, professional, doctorate
Share of total consumer units	**100.0%**	**13.1%**	**24.9%**	**20.6%**	**9.9%**	**31.5%**	**19.9%**	**11.6%**
Share of total before-tax income	**100.0**	**6.6**	**17.9**	**17.6**	**10.0**	**47.9**	**27.2**	**20.7**
Share of total spending	**100.0**	**7.9**	**19.4**	**18.5**	**10.1**	**44.1**	**25.7**	**18.4**
Pets	**100.0**	**7.6**	**20.4**	**21.0**	**14.3**	**36.3**	**20.8**	**15.5**
Pet food	100.0	10.6	22.8	20.8	16.3	29.2	17.6	11.6
Pet purchase, supplies, and medicines	100.0	9.7	20.5	21.1	12.1	36.7	21.9	14.7
Pet services	100.0	3.9	13.8	19.5	8.7	54.0	30.5	23.5
Veterinary services	100.0	2.8	19.2	21.4	15.2	40.3	21.2	19.1

Note: Numbers may not add to total because of rounding.
Source: Calculations by New Strategist based on the Bureau of Labor Statistics' 2012 Consumer Expenditure Survey

Pet Food

Best customers:	Householders aged 45 to 74
	Married couples without children at home
	Married couples with school-aged or older children at home
	Non-Hispanic whites
	Households in the West
Customer trends:	Average household spending on pet food may continue to grow
	because the large baby-boom generation is solidly in the
	best-customer age groups.

Pet food accounts for 37 percent of pet spending—a larger share than any other pet category. Householders ranging in age from 45 to 74 spend more than the average household on pet food. Married couples without children at home spend 38 percent more than average on pet food, and those with school-aged or older children at home spend 29 to 56 percent more. Non-Hispanic whites spend 18 percent more than average on pet food and control 89 percent of the market. Households in the West spend 22 percent more than average on pet food.

Average household spending on pet food rose by a steep 70 percent between 2000 and 2012, after adjusting for inflation. Spending on pet food may continue to grow because the large baby-boom generation is solidly in the best-customer age groups.

Table 32. Pet food

Total household spending	$24,223,795,200.00
Average household spends	194.70

	AVERAGE HOUSEHOLD SPENDING	BEST CUSTOMERS (index)	BIGGEST CUSTOMERS (market share)
AGE OF HOUSEHOLDER			
Average household	**$194.70**	**100**	**100.0%**
Under age 25	90.76	47	3.1
Aged 25 to 34	145.13	75	12.0
Aged 35 to 44	170.82	88	15.2
Aged 45 to 54	218.24	112	22.2
Aged 55 to 64	312.50	161	29.4
Aged 65 to 74	221.08	114	13.7
Aged 75 or older	96.97	50	4.9

	AVERAGE HOUSEHOLD SPENDING	BEST CUSTOMERS (index)	BIGGEST CUSTOMERS (market share)
HOUSEHOLD INCOME			
Average household	**$194.70**	**100**	**100.0%**
Under $20,000	85.39	44	9.2
$20,000 to $39,999	148.98	77	17.2
$40,000 to $49,999	172.68	89	7.8
$50,000 to $69,999	192.28	99	14.3
$70,000 to $79,999	273.89	141	7.9
$80,000 to $99,999	249.11	128	11.3
$100,000 or more	333.99	172	32.1
HOUSEHOLD TYPE			
Average household	**194.70**	**100**	**100.0**
Married couples	262.85	135	65.6
Married couples, no children	269.46	138	28.9
Married couples with children	267.39	137	32.3
Oldest child under age 6	196.26	101	4.6
Oldest child aged 6 to 17	303.34	156	18.5
Oldest child aged 18 or older	251.76	129	9.1
Single parent with child under age 18	100.71	52	2.7
Single person	124.04	64	18.9
RACE AND HISPANIC ORIGIN			
Average household	**194.70**	**100**	**100.0**
Asian	76.44	39	1.7
Black	59.90	31	3.9
Hispanic	116.46	60	7.5
Non-Hispanic white and other	230.12	118	88.7
REGION			
Average household	**194.70**	**100**	**100.0**
Northeast	175.51	90	16.3
Midwest	202.04	104	23.0
South	173.54	89	33.2
West	238.09	122	27.6
EDUCATION			
Average household	**194.70**	**100**	**100.0**
Less than high school graduate	157.31	81	10.6
High school graduate	177.68	91	22.8
Some college	197.10	101	20.8
Associate's degree	321.85	165	16.3
Bachelor's degree or more	180.52	93	29.2
Bachelor's degree	172.22	88	17.6
Master's, professional, doctoral degree	194.55	100	11.6

Note: Market shares may not sum to 100.0 because of rounding and missing categories by household type. "Asian" and "black" include Hispanics and non-Hispanics who identify themselves as being of the respective race alone. "Hispanic" includes people of any race who identify themselves as Hispanic. "Other" includes people who identify themselves as non-Hispanic and as Alaska Native, American Indian, Asian (who are also included in the "Asian" row), or Native Hawaiian or other Pacific Islander, as well as non-Hispanics reporting more than one race.
Source: Calculations by New Strategist based on the Bureau of Labor Statistics' 2012 Consumer Expenditure Survey

Pet Purchase, Supplies, and Medicines

Best customers: Householders aged 35 to 64
                          Married couples without children at home
                          Married couples with school-aged or older children at home
                          Non-Hispanic whites

Customer trends: Average household spending on pet purchases, supplies, and
                          medicines may stabilize in the years ahead along with the cost of
                          pet medications.

Pets are so popular in the United States that spending on pet purchase, supplies, and medicines does not vary much by demographic characteristic, except by race and Hispanic origin. Householders ranging in age from 35 to 64 spend 14 to 36 percent more than average on pet purchase, supplies, medicines. Married couples spend 25 percent more, the figure peaking at 40 percent among couples with school-aged children. To understand the market, it is almost more helpful to know who is least likely to spend on pets—single parents, people who live alone, low-income households, the youngest and the oldest householders, and minority householders all spend considerably less than average on pet purchase, supplies, and medicines.

Average household spending on pet purchase, supplies, and medicines more than tripled between 2000 and 2010, after adjusting for inflation, as pharmaceutical companies offered a growing variety of pricey medications. Between 2010 and 2012, however, spending on this category fell 21 percent as consumers reacted to the shock of higher pet costs by searching for substitutes and as greater competition reduced the price of medications. Average household spending on pet purchase, supplies, and medicines may stabilize in the years ahead along with the cost of pet medications.

Table 33. Pet purchase, supplies, and medicines

Total household spending $16,882,007,040.00
Average household spends   135.69

	AVERAGE HOUSEHOLD SPENDING	BEST CUSTOMERS (index)	BIGGEST CUSTOMERS (market share)
AGE OF HOUSEHOLDER			
Average household	**$135.69**	**100**	**100.0%**
Under age 25	73.78	54	3.6
Aged 25 to 34	124.11	91	14.8
Aged 35 to 44	161.02	119	20.6
Aged 45 to 54	184.48	136	26.9
Aged 55 to 64	154.95	114	20.9
Aged 65 to 74	108.26	80	9.6
Aged 75 or older	50.35	37	3.6

	AVERAGE HOUSEHOLD SPENDING	BEST CUSTOMERS (index)	BIGGEST CUSTOMERS (market share)
HOUSEHOLD INCOME			
Average household	**$135.69**	**100**	**100.0%**
Under $20,000	60.34	44	9.4
$20,000 to $39,999	99.82	74	16.6
$40,000 to $49,999	120.97	89	7.9
$50,000 to $69,999	133.64	98	14.2
$70,000 to $79,999	167.33	123	6.9
$80,000 to $99,999	219.65	162	14.3
$100,000 or more	223.08	164	30.8
HOUSEHOLD TYPE			
Average household	**135.69**	**100**	**100.0**
Married couples	169.31	125	60.6
Married couples, no children	161.47	119	24.8
Married couples with children	172.05	127	29.8
Oldest child under age 6	117.47	87	3.9
Oldest child aged 6 to 17	189.29	140	16.6
Oldest child aged 18 or older	178.29	131	9.3
Single parent with child under age 18	107.18	79	4.1
Single person	80.99	60	17.7
RACE AND HISPANIC ORIGIN			
Average household	**135.69**	**100**	**100.0**
Asian	51.84	38	1.7
Black	46.12	34	4.3
Hispanic	82.95	61	7.7
Non-Hispanic white and other	159.29	117	88.1
REGION			
Average household	**135.69**	**100**	**100.0**
Northeast	133.56	98	17.8
Midwest	137.71	101	22.5
South	142.20	105	39.0
West	124.65	92	20.7
EDUCATION			
Average household	**135.69**	**100**	**100.0**
Less than high school graduate	101.02	74	9.7
High school graduate	111.29	82	20.5
Some college	139.04	102	21.1
Associate's degree	165.80	122	12.1
Bachelor's degree or more	157.72	116	36.7
Bachelor's degree	149.43	110	21.9
Master's, professional, doctoral degree	171.95	127	14.7

Note: Market shares may not sum to 100.0 because of rounding and missing categories by household type. "Asian" and "black" include Hispanics and non-Hispanics who identify themselves as being of the respective race alone. "Hispanic" includes people of any race who identify themselves as Hispanic. "Other" includes people who identify themselves as non-Hispanic and as Alaska Native, American Indian, Asian (who are also included in the "Asian" row), or Native Hawaiian or other Pacific Islander, as well as non-Hispanics reporting more than one race.
Source: Calculations by New Strategist based on the Bureau of Labor Statistics' 2012 Consumer Expenditure Survey

Pet Services

Best customers: Householders aged 45 to 64

Married couples without children at home

Married couples with children under age 18

Non-Hispanic whites

Households in the West

Customer trends: Average household spending on pet services is likely to stabilize or even decline in the years ahead as the large baby-boom generation retires.

The best customers of pet services—such as dog walking and day care—are busy, working adults. Householders ranging in age from 45 to 64 spend 50 to 51 percent more than average on this item. Married couples without children at home (most of them empty-nesters) spend two-thirds more than average on pet services, while those with school-aged or younger children spend 28 to 45 percent more than average. Non-Hispanic whites outspend minorities by a large margin and account for 91 percent of the market. Households in the West spend 20 percent more than average on pet services.

Average household spending on pet services rose 62 percent between 2000 and 2012, after adjusting for inflation, as the baby-boom generation filled the best-customer life stage and day care services for dogs became more popular. Spending on pet services is likely to stabilize or even decline in the years ahead as the large baby-boom generation retires.

Table 34. Pet services

Total household spending	$5,188,147,200.00
Average household spends	41.70

	AVERAGE HOUSEHOLD SPENDING	BEST CUSTOMERS (index)	BIGGEST CUSTOMERS (market share)
AGE OF HOUSEHOLDER			
Average household	**$41.70**	**100**	**100.0%**
Under age 25	8.24	20	1.3
Aged 25 to 34	31.70	76	12.3
Aged 35 to 44	39.42	95	16.4
Aged 45 to 54	62.54	150	29.7
Aged 55 to 64	62.97	151	27.6
Aged 65 to 74	32.10	77	9.3
Aged 75 or older	14.55	35	3.4

	AVERAGE HOUSEHOLD SPENDING	BEST CUSTOMERS (index)	BIGGEST CUSTOMERS (market share)
HOUSEHOLD INCOME			
Average household	**$41.70**	**100**	**100.0%**
Under $20,000	11.69	28	5.9
$20,000 to $39,999	17.66	42	9.5
$40,000 to $49,999	20.35	49	4.3
$50,000 to $69,999	40.99	98	14.2
$70,000 to $79,999	36.13	87	4.8
$80,000 to $99,999	69.29	166	14.7
$100,000 or more	103.66	249	46.5
HOUSEHOLD TYPE			
Average household	**41.70**	**100**	**100.0**
Married couples	59.21	142	69.0
Married couples, no children	69.22	166	34.6
Married couples with children	55.05	132	31.0
Oldest child under age 6	53.29	128	5.8
Oldest child aged 6 to 17	60.31	145	17.2
Oldest child aged 18 or older	47.31	113	8.0
Single parent with child under age 18	27.61	66	3.5
Single person	26.09	63	18.6
RACE AND HISPANIC ORIGIN			
Average household	**41.70**	**100**	**100.0**
Asian	12.07	29	1.3
Black	9.14	22	2.8
Hispanic	19.48	47	5.9
Non-Hispanic white and other	50.82	122	91.5
REGION			
Average household	**41.70**	**100**	**100.0**
Northeast	40.19	96	17.4
Midwest	42.29	101	22.5
South	36.98	89	33.0
West	50.13	120	27.1
EDUCATION			
Average household	**41.70**	**100**	**100.0**
Less than high school graduate	12.54	30	3.9
High school graduate	23.10	55	13.8
Some college	39.53	95	19.5
Associate's degree	36.85	88	8.7
Bachelor's degree or more	71.41	171	54.0
Bachelor's degree	63.85	153	30.5
Master's, professional, doctoral degree	84.39	202	23.5

Note: Market shares may not sum to 100.0 because of rounding and missing categories by household type. "Asian" and "black" include Hispanics and non-Hispanics who identify themselves as being of the respective race alone. "Hispanic" includes people of any race who identify themselves as Hispanic. "Other" includes people who identify themselves as non-Hispanic and as Alaska Native, American Indian, Asian (who are also included in the "Asian" row), or Native Hawaiian or other Pacific Islander, as well as non-Hispanics reporting more than one race.
Source: Calculations by New Strategist based on the Bureau of Labor Statistics' 2012 Consumer Expenditure Survey

Veterinary Services

Best customers:
Householders aged 55 to 74
Married couples without children at home
Married couples with school-aged or older children at home
Non-Hispanic whites

Customer trends:
Average household spending on veterinary services should continue to grow in the years ahead as the large baby-boom generation fills the best-customer age groups.

The best customers of veterinary services are older married couples, many of whom have older pets that require extensive veterinary care. Householders aged 55 to 74 spend 35 to 40 percent more than average on veterinary services. Married couples with school-aged or older children at home spend 45 to 48 percent more than average on veterinary services, and those without children at home (many of them older empty nesters) spend 49 percent more. Non-Hispanic whites dominate this category, spending 26 percent more than average.

Average household spending on veterinary services grew by an enormous 70 percent between 2000 and 2012, after adjusting for inflation. Spending on veterinary services should continue to grow in the years ahead as the large baby-boom generation fills the best-customer age groups.

Table 35. Veterinary services

| Total household spending | $18,656,179,200.00 |
| Average household spends | 149.95 |

	AVERAGE HOUSEHOLD SPENDING	BEST CUSTOMERS (index)	BIGGEST CUSTOMERS (market share)
AGE OF HOUSEHOLDER			
Average household	**$149.95**	**100**	**100.0%**
Under age 25	12.07	8	0.5
Aged 25 to 34	102.42	68	11.0
Aged 35 to 44	142.36	95	16.5
Aged 45 to 54	155.13	103	20.5
Aged 55 to 64	209.47	140	25.6
Aged 65 to 74	202.80	135	16.3
Aged 75 or older	157.23	105	10.2

	AVERAGE HOUSEHOLD SPENDING	BEST CUSTOMERS (index)	BIGGEST CUSTOMERS (market share)
HOUSEHOLD INCOME			
Average household	**$149.95**	**100**	**100.0%**
Under $20,000	49.89	33	7.0
$20,000 to $39,999	146.99	98	22.1
$40,000 to $49,999	24.25	16	1.4
$50,000 to $69,999	153.07	102	14.7
$70,000 to $79,999	176.46	118	6.6
$80,000 to $99,999	173.64	116	10.2
$100,000 or more	308.45	206	38.5
HOUSEHOLD TYPE			
Average household	**149.95**	**100**	**100.0**
Married couples	210.93	141	68.3
Married couples, no children	223.36	149	31.1
Married couples with children	195.57	130	30.7
Oldest child under age 6	89.50	60	2.7
Oldest child aged 6 to 17	222.35	148	17.6
Oldest child aged 18 or older	216.99	145	10.2
Single parent with child under age 18	44.00	29	1.5
Single person	85.56	57	16.9
RACE AND HISPANIC ORIGIN			
Average household	**149.95**	**100**	**100.0**
Asian	21.13	14	0.6
Black	30.84	21	2.6
Hispanic	34.20	23	2.9
Non-Hispanic white and other	188.98	126	94.6
REGION			
Average household	**149.95**	**100**	**100.0**
Northeast	142.67	95	17.2
Midwest	136.58	91	20.2
South	169.79	113	42.2
West	136.29	91	20.5
EDUCATION			
Average household	**149.95**	**100**	**100.0**
Less than high school graduate	31.69	21	2.8
High school graduate	115.52	77	19.2
Some college	155.78	104	21.4
Associate's degree	230.71	154	15.2
Bachelor's degree or more	191.79	128	40.3
Bachelor's degree	159.18	106	21.2
Master's, professional, doctoral degree	246.90	165	19.1

Note: Market shares may not sum to 100.0 because of rounding and missing categories by household type. "Asian" and "black" include Hispanics and non-Hispanics who identify themselves as being of the respective race alone. "Hispanic" includes people of any race who identify themselves as Hispanic. "Other" includes people who identify themselves as non-Hispanic and as Alaska Native, American Indian, Asian (who are also included in the "Asian" row), or Native Hawaiian or other Pacific Islander, as well as non-Hispanics reporting more than one race.
Source: Calculations by New Strategist based on the Bureau of Labor Statistics' 2012 Consumer Expenditure Survey

Appendix

Spending by Product and Service Ranked by Amount Spent, 2012

(average annual spending of consumer units on products and services, ranked by amount spent, 2012)

1.	Deductions for Social Security	$4,040.62
2.	Groceries (also shown by individual category)	3,920.65
3.	Vehicle purchases (net outlay)	3,210.49
4.	Mortgage interest (or rent, $3,064.09)	2,926.47
5.	Gasoline and motor oil	2,755.78
6.	Restaurants (also shown by meal category)	2,225.50
7.	Health insurance	2,060.78
8.	Property taxes	1,835.60
9.	Federal income taxes	1,568.33
10.	Electricity	1,387.83
11.	Dinner at restaurants	1,082.12
12.	Vehicle insurance	1,017.94
13.	Cellular phone service	861.97
14.	College tuition	824.99
15.	Vehicle maintenance and repairs	814.27
16.	Lunch at restaurants	746.81
17.	Cash contributions to church, religious organizations	734.30
18.	Cable and satellite television services	661.76
19.	Nonpayroll deposit to retirement plans	582.46
20.	Maintenance and repair services, owner	578.78
21.	Women's apparel	572.53
22.	State and local income taxes	526.08
23.	Deductions for private pensions	511.80
24.	Cash gifts to members of other households	464.50
25.	Alcoholic beverages	451.16
26.	Water and sewerage maintenance	398.56
27.	Prescription drugs	366.40
28.	Natural gas	359.35
29.	Residential telephone service and pay phones	358.54
30.	Homeowner's insurance	353.80
31.	Life and other personal insurance	352.61
32.	Airline fares	352.53
33.	Lodging on trips	341.61
34.	Computer information services	336.30
35.	Men's apparel	319.73
36.	Cigarettes	298.75
37.	Personal care services	292.83
38.	Dental services	268.32
39.	Fresh fruits	261.29
40.	Restaurant meals on trips	257.15
41.	Day care centers, nurseries, and preschools	236.56
42.	Cash contributions to charities	233.63
43.	Owned vacation homes	230.28
44.	Breakfast at restaurants	227.60
45.	Beef	226.32
46.	Fresh vegetables	226.14
47.	Vehicle finance charges	223.36
48.	Child support expenditures	208.46
49.	Physician's services	204.16
50.	Pet food	194.70

51.	Finance charges, except mortgage and vehicles	$181.53
52.	Elementary and high school tuition	169.04
53.	Snacks at restaurants	168.97
54.	Movie, theater, amusement park, and other admissions	168.75
55.	Pork	165.77
56.	Computers and computer hardware for nonbusiness use	162.71
57.	Hospital room and services	161.48
58.	Poultry	159.36
59.	Women's footwear	158.87
60.	Leased vehicles	158.68
61.	Cosmetics, perfume, and bath products	157.04
62.	Laundry and cleaning supplies	155.39
63.	Veterinarian services	149.95
64.	Expenses for other properties	149.93
65.	Prepared foods except frozen, salads, and desserts	147.81
66.	Interest paid, home equity loan/line of credit	140.37
67.	Carbonated drinks	139.74
68.	Legal fees	138.71
69.	Pet purchase, supplies, and medicines	135.69
70.	Other taxes	131.96
71.	Housekeeping services	131.93
72.	Cheese	131.47
73.	Fresh milk, all types	128.28
74.	Social, recreation, health club membership	127.44
75.	Household decorative items	126.84
76.	Fish and seafood	125.74
77.	Gardening, lawn care service	125.40
78.	Miscellaneous household products	125.00
79.	Trash and garbage collection	123.44
80.	Fees for participant sports	118.19
81.	Cleansing and toilet tissue, paper towels, and napkins	117.50
82.	Girls' (aged 2 to 15) apparel	115.92
83.	Toys, games, hobbies, and tricycles	114.59
84.	Beer and ale at home	112.49
85.	Men's footwear	111.75
86.	Potato chips and other snacks	111.59
87.	Vehicle registration	111.25
88.	Support for college students	104.82
89.	Wine at home	102.62
90.	Television sets	102.24
91.	Sofas	101.36
92.	Deductions for government retirement	100.54
93.	Nonprescription drugs	97.49
94.	Ready-to-eat and cooked cereals	94.82
95.	Jewelry	94.38
96.	Fees for recreational lessons	92.55
97.	Boys' (aged 2 to 15) apparel	87.96
98.	Candy and chewing gum	87.86
99.	Lunch meats (cold cuts)	87.23
100.	Coffee	86.50
101.	Maintenance and repair materials, owner	86.31
102.	Alimony expenditures	86.01
103.	Babysitting and child care	84.86
104.	Rent as pay	84.60
105.	Fuel oil	80.77
106.	Housing while attending school	76.65
107.	Mattresses and springs	76.43
108.	Lawn and garden supplies	76.04
109.	Beer and ale at bars, restaurants	75.94
110.	Stationery, stationery supplies, giftwrap	75.07

111.	Accounting fees	$75.03
112.	Funeral expenses	72.17
113.	Intracity mass transit fares	71.99
114.	Lawn and garden equipment	71.11
115.	Frozen prepared foods, except meals	70.22
116.	Bedroom linens	67.43
117.	Eyeglasses and contact lenses	66.52
118.	Motorized recreational vehicles	65.66
119.	Admission to sports events	65.45
120.	Books and supplies for college	65.30
121.	Children's (under age 2) apparel	63.31
122.	Bedroom furniture except mattresses and springs	63.24
123.	Service by professionals other than physician	62.38
124.	Hair care products	61.69
125.	Bread, other than white	61.60
126.	Athletic gear, game tables, exercise equipment	60.99
127.	Frozen meals	60.61
128.	Sauces and gravies	60.27
129.	Catered affairs	60.19
130.	Refrigerators and freezers	59.80
131.	School lunches	59.56
132.	Ground rent	58.68
133.	Lottery and gambling losses	57.93
134.	Postage	57.44
135.	Ice cream and related products	57.37
136.	Moving, storage, and freight express	56.88
137.	Bottled water	56.80
138.	Ship fares	56.53
139.	School tuition, books, and supplies other than college, vocational/technical, elementary, high school	55.30
140.	Canned and bottled fruit juice	54.92
141.	Canned vegetables	54.59
142.	Indoor plants and fresh flowers	53.57
143.	Property management, owner	53.28
144.	Eggs	53.08
145.	Other dairy (yogurt, etc.)	52.67
146.	Professional laundry, dry cleaning	52.24
147.	Biscuits and rolls	51.85
148.	Nonprescription vitamins	50.76
149.	Cookies	50.56
150.	Food prepared by consumer unit on trips	50.23
151.	Occupational expenses	48.41
152.	Bottled gas	47.44
153.	Other alcoholic beverages at bars, restaurants	47.43
154.	Lab tests, X-rays	46.91
155.	Canned and packaged soups	46.30
156.	Books	45.30
157.	Board (including at school)	44.93
158.	Alcoholic beverages purchased on trips	43.80
159.	White bread	43.52
160.	Care for elderly, invalids, handicapped, etc.	43.36
161.	Wall units, cabinets, and other furniture	42.39
162.	Nuts	42.35
163.	Parking fees	42.29
164.	Unmotored recreational vehicles	42.12
165.	Eye care services	41.86
166.	Pet services	41.70
167.	Topicals and dressings	40.99
168.	Oral hygiene products	40.82
169.	Coin-operated apparel laundry and dry cleaning	40.21

170.	Newspaper and magazine subscriptions	$39.58
171.	Power tools	39.34
172.	Boys' footwear	39.09
173.	Miscellaneous personal services	38.97
174.	Cash contributions to educational institutions	38.77
175.	Salt, spices, and other seasonings	38.72
176.	Cakes and cupcakes	37.94
177.	Frozen vegetables	37.50
178.	Crackers	37.17
179.	Girls' footwear	37.12
180.	Video game hardware and accessories	37.03
181.	Pasta, cornmeal, and other cereal products	36.98
182.	Fats and oils	36.79
183.	Rented vehicles	36.23
184.	Tolls	35.63
185.	Prepared salads	35.09
186.	Living room chairs	34.57
187.	Care in convalescent or nursing home	34.56
188.	Wine at bars, restaurants	34.54
189.	Deodorants, feminine hygiene, miscellaneous products	34.51
190.	Washing machines	34.12
191.	Sound components, equipment, and accessories	32.07
192.	Kitchen and dining room furniture	31.62
193.	Salad dressings	31.29
194.	Photographic equipment	31.17
195.	Meals as pay	30.79
196.	Tea	30.36
197.	Tobacco products other than cigarettes	30.30
198.	Video cassettes, tapes, and discs	29.70
199.	Jams, preserves, other sweets	29.61
200.	Hunting and fishing equipment	29.06
201.	Frozen and refrigerated bakery products	28.77
202.	Telephones and accessories	27.33
203.	Home security system service fee	27.23
204.	Lamps and lighting fixtures	26.83
205.	Small electric kitchen appliances	25.90
206.	Noncarbonated fruit-flavored drinks	25.83
207.	Butter	25.56
208.	Baby food	25.05
209.	Baking needs	24.95
210.	Cash contributions to political organizations	24.90
211.	Frankfurters	24.71
212.	Rice	24.65
213.	Termite and pest control products and services	24.58
214.	Outdoor equipment	24.51
215.	Sugar	24.38
216.	Clothes dryers	23.95
217.	Bathroom linens	23.90
218.	Sweetrolls, coffee cakes, doughnuts	23.73
219.	Cooking stoves, ovens	23.67
220.	Cream	23.58
221.	Checking accounts, other bank service charges	23.10
222.	Bicycles	21.69
223.	Other alcoholic beverages at home	21.40
224.	Hearing aids	21.23
225.	Photographer fees	21.12
226.	Nonclothing laundry and dry cleaning, sent out	21.09
227.	Recreation expenses on trips	20.99
228.	Canned fruits	20.35
229.	Automobile service clubs	20.09

230.	Laundry and cleaning equipment	$19.59
231.	Outdoor furniture	19.36
232.	Shaving products	19.18
233.	Vegetable juices	18.98
234.	Tableware, nonelectric kitchenware	18.89
235.	Intercity train fares	18.88
236.	Nonelectric cookware	18.86
237.	Peanut butter	18.68
238.	Nondairy cream and imitation milk	18.59
239.	Dried vegetables	18.22
240.	Local transportation on trips	17.81
241.	Olives, pickles, relishes	17.46
242.	Gifts of stocks, bonds, and mutual funds to members of other households	17.16
243.	Fresh fruit juice	17.06
244.	Musical instruments and accessories	16.80
245.	Dishwashers (built-in), garbage disposals, range hoods	16.61
246.	Books and supplies for elementary and high school	16.25
247.	Floor coverings	16.22
248.	Prepared flour mixes	16.18
249.	Electric floor-cleaning equipment	16.07
250.	Test preparation, tutoring services	15.86
251.	Computer accessories	15.85
252.	Rental of video cassettes, tapes, discs, films	15.72
253.	Maintenance and repair services, renter	15.71
254.	Nonalcoholic beverages (except carbonated, coffee, fruit-flavored drinks, and tea) and ice	15.36
255.	Appliance repair, including at service center	15.36
256.	Sports drinks	15.12
257.	Watches	15.09
258.	Computer software	15.04
259.	Satellite radio service	14.83
260.	Tenant's insurance	14.74
261.	Window coverings	14.64
262.	Prepared desserts	14.29
263.	Luggage	13.79
264.	Digital book readers	13.62
265.	Security services, owner	13.56
266.	Infants' equipment	13.42
267.	Pies, tarts, turnovers	13.41
268.	Cemetery lots, vaults, and maintenance fees	13.16
269.	Whiskey at home	12.93
270.	Living room tables	12.92
271.	Rental of party supplies for catered affairs	12.63
272.	Closet and storage items	12.60
273.	Intercity bus fares	11.96
274.	Vehicle inspection	11.85
275.	Hand tools	11.79
276.	Compact discs, records, and audio tapes	11.78
277.	Driver's license	11.64
278.	Taxi fares and limousine service	11.36
279.	Camping equipment	11.06
280.	Newspapers and magazines, nonsubscription	10.88
281.	Microwave ovens	10.55
282.	Streamed and downloaded audio	10.39
283.	Electric personal care appliances	10.39
284.	Lamb, organ meats, and others	10.19
285.	Shopping club membership fees	10.16
286.	Curtains and draperies	9.88
287.	Voice over IP	9.64

288.	Infants' furniture	$9.59
289.	Flour	9.36
290.	Photo processing	9.15
291.	Phone cards	9.00
292.	Hair accessories	8.92
293.	Parking at owned home	8.87
294.	Portable heating and cooling equipment	8.84
295.	Stamp and coin collecting	8.80
296.	China and other dinnerware	8.76
297.	Margarine	8.74
298.	Material for making clothes	8.74
299.	Coal, wood, and other fuels	8.72
300.	Dried fruits	8.71
301.	Sewing materials for household items	8.48
302.	Internet services away from home	8.25
303.	Kitchen and dining room linens	8.15
304.	Miscellaneous video equipment	8.08
305.	Glassware	7.94
306.	Repairs and rentals of lawn and garden equipment, hand and power tools, etc.	7.90
307.	Vocational and technical school tuition	7.66
308.	Docking and landing fees	7.45
309.	Personal digital audio players	7.41
310.	Vacation clubs	7.38
311.	VCRs and video disc players	7.35
312.	Bread and cracker products	7.31
313.	Frozen fruits	7.16
314.	Maintenance and repair materials, renter	7.12
315.	Live entertainment for catered affairs	6.48
316.	Rental of recreational vehicles	6.11
317.	Apparel alteration, repair, and tailoring services	6.03
318.	Office furniture for home use	6.02
319.	Global positioning system devices	5.66
320.	Frozen fruit juices	5.55
321.	Repair of computer systems for nonbusiness use	5.52
322.	Streamed and downloaded video	5.35
323.	Medical equipment for general use	5.16
324.	Window air conditioners	4.95
325.	Artificial sweeteners	4.91
326.	Nonclothing laundry and dry cleaning, coin-operated	4.79
327.	Watch and jewelry repair	4.72
328.	Personal digital assistants	4.70
329.	Water sports equipment	4.45
330.	Rental of furniture	4.44
331.	Towing charges	4.37
332.	Water-softening service	4.30
333.	Sewing patterns and notions	4.20
334.	Winter sports equipment	4.19
335.	Slipcovers and decorative pillows	3.94
336.	Applications, games, ringtones for handheld devices	3.86
337.	Portable memory	3.76
338.	Business equipment for home use	3.63
339.	Online gaming services	3.51
340.	Supportive and convalescent medical equipment	3.48
341.	Delivery services	3.43
342.	Safe deposit box rental	3.36
343.	Video game software	3.26
344.	Reupholstering and furniture repair	3.21
345.	Repair of TV, radio, and sound equipment	3.09
346.	Septic tank cleaning	2.95

347.	Flatware	$2.93
348.	Credit card memberships	2.92
349.	Deductions for railroad retirement	2.89
350.	Adult diapers	2.86
351.	Playground equipment	2.84
352.	Wigs and hairpieces	2.82
353.	Plastic dinnerware	2.68
354.	Smoking accessories	2.68
355.	Sewing machines	2.54
356.	Fireworks	2.46
357.	Global positioning services	2.06
358.	Silver serving pieces	2.04
359.	Rental and repair of miscellaneous sports equipment	1.86
360.	Pinball, electronic video games	1.78
361.	Smoke alarms	1.75
362.	Rental and repair of musical instruments	1.70
363.	Clothing rental	1.69
364.	Rental of medical equipment	1.53
365.	Shoe repair and other shoe services	1.52
366.	Appliance rental	1.50
367.	Satellite dishes	1.24
368.	School bus	1.15
369.	Other serving pieces	1.04
370.	Installation of television sets	0.74
371.	Books and supplies for vocational and technical schools	0.71
372.	Clothing storage	0.70
373.	Rental of office equipment for nonbusiness use	0.68
374.	Rental of supportive and convalescent medical equipment	0.68
375.	Telephone answering devices	0.59
376.	Dating services	0.50
377.	Installation of computer	0.44
378.	Repair and rental of photographic equipment	0.39
379.	Books and supplies for day care and nursery	0.38

Source: Calculations by New Strategist based on the Bureau of Labor Statistics' 2012 Consumer Expenditure Survey

Glossary

age The age of the reference person.

alcoholic beverages Includes beer and ale, wine, whiskey, gin, vodka, rum, and other alcoholic beverages.

annual spending The annual amount spent per household. The Bureau of Labor Statistics calculates the annual average for all households in a segment, not just for those that purchased an item. The averages are calculated by integrating the results of the diary (weekly) and interview (quarterly) portions of the Consumer Expenditure Survey. For items purchased by most households—such as bread—average annual spending figures are a fairly accurate account of actual spending. For products and services purchased by few households during a year's time—such as cars—the average annual amount spent is much less than what purchasers spend.

apparel, accessories, and related services Includes the following:

men's and boys' apparel Includes coats, jackets, sweaters, vests, sport coats, tailored jackets, slacks, shorts and short sets, sportswear, shirts, underwear, nightwear, hosiery, uniforms, and other accessories.

women's and girls' apparel Includes coats, jackets, furs, sport coats, tailored jackets, sweaters, vests, blouses, shirts, dresses, dungarees, culottes, slacks, shorts, sportswear, underwear, nightwear, uniforms, hosiery, and other accessories.

infants' apparel Includes coats, jackets, snowsuits, underwear, diapers, dresses, crawlers, sleeping garments, hosiery, footwear, and other accessories for children.

footwear Includes articles such as shoes, slippers, boots, and other similar items. It excludes footwear for babies and footwear used for sports such as bowling or golf shoes.

other apparel products and services Includes material for making clothes, shoe repair, alterations and sewing patterns and notions, clothing rental, clothing storage, dry cleaning, sent-out laundry, watches, jewelry, and repairs to watches and jewelry.

baby boom Americans born between 1946 and 1964.

cash contributions Includes cash contributed to persons or organizations outside the consumer unit including court-ordered alimony, child support payments, support for college students, and contributions to religious, educational, charitable, or political organizations.

consumer unit (1) All members of a household who are related by blood, marriage, adoption, or other legal arrangements; (2) a person living alone or sharing a household with others or living as a roomer in a private home or lodging house or in permanent living quarters in a hotel or motel, but who is financially independent; or (3) two or more persons living together who pool their income to make joint expenditure decisions. Financial independence is determined by the three major expense categories: housing, food, and other living expenses. To be considered financially independent, at least two of the three major expense categories have to be provided by the respondent. For convenience, called household in the text of this report.

consumer unit, composition of The classification of interview households by type according to (1) relationship of other household members to the reference person; (2) age of the children of the reference person; and (3) combination of relationship to the reference person and age of the children. Stepchildren and adopted children are included with the reference person's own children.

earner A consumer unit member aged 14 or older who worked at least one week during the 12 months prior to the interview date.

education Includes tuition, fees, books, supplies, and equipment for public and private nursery schools, elementary and high schools, colleges and universities, and other schools.

entertainment Includes the following:

• fees and admissions Includes fees for participant sports; admissions to sporting events, movies, concerts, plays; health, swimming, tennis, and country club memberships, and other social recreational and fraternal organizations; recreational lessons or instructions; and recreational expenses on trips.

• audio and visual equipment and services Includes television sets; radios; cable TV; tape recorders and players; video cassettes, tapes, and discs; video cassette recorders and video disc players; video game hardware and software; personal digital audio players; streaming and downloading audio and video; sound components; CDs, records, and tapes; musical instruments; and rental and repair of TV and sound equipment.

• pets, toys, hobbies, and playground equipment Includes pet food, pet services, veterinary expenses, toys, games, hobbies, and playground equipment.

• other entertainment equipment and services Includes indoor exercise equipment, athletic shoes, bicycles, trailers, campers, camping equipment, rental of campers and trailers, hunting and fishing equipment, sports equipment, winter sports equipment, water sports equipment, boats, boat motors and boat trailers, rental of boats, landing and docking fees, rental and repair of sports equipment, photographic equipment, film, photo processing, photographer fees, repair and rental of photo equipment, fireworks, pinball and electronic video games.

expenditure The transaction cost including excise and sales taxes of goods and services acquired during the survey period. The full cost of each purchase is recorded even though full payment may not have been made at the date of purchase. Expenditure estimates include gifts. Excluded from expenditures are purchases or portions of purchases directly assignable to business purposes and periodic credit or installment payments on goods and services already acquired.

federal income tax Includes federal income tax withheld in the survey year to pay for income earned in survey year plus additional tax paid in survey year to cover any underpayment or underwithholding of tax in the year prior to the survey.

financial products and services Includes accounting fees, legal fees, union dues, professional dues and fees, other occupational expenses, funerals, cemetery lots, dating services, shopping club memberships, and unclassified fees and personal services.

food Includes the following:

• food at home Refers to the total expenditures for food at grocery stores or other food stores during the interview period. It is calculated by multiplying the number of visits to a grocery or other food store by the average amount spent per visit. It excludes the purchase of nonfood items.

• food away from home Includes all meals (breakfast, lunch, brunch, and dinner) at restaurants, carry-outs, and vending machines, including tips, plus meals as pay, special catered affairs such as weddings, bar mitzvahs, and confirmations, and meals away from home on trips.

generation X Americans born between 1965 and 1976. Also known as the baby-bust generation.

gifts for people in other households Includes gift expenditures for people living in other consumer units. The amount spent on gifts is also included in individual product and service categories.

health care Includes the following:

• *health insurance* Includes health maintenance plans (HMOs), Blue Cross/Blue Shield, commercial health insurance, Medicare, Medicare supplemental insurance, long-term care insurance, and other health insurance.

• *medical services* Includes hospital room and services, physicians' services, services of a practitioner other than a physician, eye and dental care, lab tests, X-rays, nursing, therapy services, care in convalescent or nursing home, and other medical care.

• *drugs* Includes prescription and nonprescription drugs, internal and respiratory over-the-counter drugs.

• *medical supplies* Includes eyeglasses and contact lenses, topicals and dressings, antiseptics, bandages, cotton, first aid kits, contraceptives; medical equipment for general use such as syringes, ice bags, thermometers, vaporizers, heating pads; supportive or convalescent medical equipment such as hearing aids, braces, canes, crutches, and walkers.

Hispanic origin The self-identified Hispanic origin of the consumer unit reference person. All consumer units are included in one of two Hispanic origin groups based on the reference person's Hispanic origin: Hispanic or non-Hispanic. Hispanics may be of any race.

household According to the Census Bureau, all the people who occupy a household. A group of unrelated people who share a housing unit as roommates or unmarried partners is also counted as a household. Households do not include group quarters such as college dormitories, prisons, or nursing homes. A household may contain more than one consumer unit. The terms "household" and "consumer unit" are used interchangeably in this report.

household furnishings and equipment Includes the following:

• *household textiles* Includes bathroom, kitchen, dining room, and other linens, curtains and drapes, slipcovers and decorative pillows, and sewing materials.

• *furniture* Includes living room, dining room, kitchen, bedroom, nursery, porch, lawn, and other outdoor furniture.

• *carpet, rugs, and other floor coverings* Includes installation and replacement of wall-to-wall carpets, room-size rugs, and other soft floor coverings.

• *major appliances* Includes refrigerators, freezers, dishwashers, stoves, ovens, garbage disposals, vacuum cleaners, microwave ovens, air-conditioners, sewing machines, washing machines, clothes dryers, and floor-cleaning equipment.

• *small appliances and miscellaneous housewares* Includes small electrical kitchen appliances, portable heating and cooling equipment, china and other dinnerware, flatware, glassware, silver and other serving pieces, nonelectric cookware, and plastic dinnerware. Excludes personal care appliances.

• *miscellaneous household equipment* Includes computer hardware and software, luggage, lamps and other lighting fixtures, window coverings, clocks, lawn mowers and gardening equipment, hand and power tools, telephone answering devices, personal digital assistants, Internet services away from home, office equipment for home use, fresh flowers and house plants, rental of furniture, closet and storage items, household decorative items, infants' equipment, outdoor equipment, smoke alarms, other household appliances, and small miscellaneous furnishing.

household services Includes the following:

• *personal services* Includes baby sitting, day care, and care of elderly and handicapped persons.

• *other household services* Includes computer information services; housekeeping services; gardening and lawn care services; coin-operated laundry and dry-cleaning of household textiles; termite and pest control products; moving, storage, and freight expenses; repair of household appliances and other household equipment; reupholstering and furniture repair; rental and repair of lawn and gardening tools; and rental of other household equipment.

housekeeping supplies Includes soaps, detergents, other laundry cleaning products, cleansing and toilet tissue, paper towels, napkins, and miscellaneous household products; lawn and garden supplies, postage stationery, stationery supplies, and gift wrap.

housing tenure "Owner" includes households living in their own homes, cooperatives, condominiums, or townhouses. "Renter" includes households paying rent as well as families living rent free in lieu of wages.

income before taxes The total money earnings and selected money receipts accruing to a consumer unit during the 12 months prior to the interview date. Income includes the following components:

• *wages and salaries* Includes total money earnings for all members of the consumer unit aged 14 or older from all jobs, including civilian wages and salaries, Armed Forces pay and allowances, piece-rate payments, commissions, tips, National Guard or Reserve pay (received for training periods), and cash bonuses before deductions for taxes, pensions, union dues, etc.

• *self-employment income* Includes net business and farm income which consists of net income (gross receipts minus operating expenses) from a profession or unincorporated business or from the operation of a farm by an owner, tenant, or sharecropper. If the business or farm is a partnership, only an appropriate share of net income is recorded. Losses are also recorded.

• *Social Security, private and government retirement* Includes payments by the federal government made under retirement, survivor, and disability insurance programs to retired persons, dependents of deceased insured workers, or to disabled workers; and private pensions or retirement benefits received by retired persons or their survivors, either directly or through an insurance company.

• *interest, dividends, rental income, and other property income* Includes interest income on savings or bonds; payments made by a corporation to its stockholders, periodic receipts from estates or trust funds; net income or loss from the rental of property, real estate, or farms, and net income or loss from roomers or boarders.

• *unemployment and workers' compensation and veterans' benefits* Includes income from unemployment compensation and workers' compensation, and veterans' payments including educational benefits but excluding military retirement.

• *public assistance, supplemental security income, and food stamps* Includes public assistance or welfare, including money received from job training grants; supplemental security income paid by federal, state, and local welfare agencies to low-income persons who are aged 65 or older, blind, or disabled; and the value of food stamps obtained.

• *regular contributions for support* Includes alimony and child support as well as any regular contributions from persons outside the consumer unit.

• *other income* Includes money income from care of foster children, cash scholarships, fellowships, or stipends not based on working; and meals and rent as pay.

indexed spending Indexed spending figures compare the spending of particular demographic segments with that of the average household. To compute an index, the amount spent on an item by a demographic segment is divided by the amount spent on the item by the average household. That figure is then multiplied by 100. An index of 100 is the average for all households. An index of 125 means average spending by households in a segment is 25 percent above average (100 plus 25). An index of 75 means average spending by households in a segment is 25 percent below average (100 minus 25). Indexed spending figures identify the consumer units that spend the most on a product or service.

life and other personal insurance Includes premiums from whole life and term insurance; endowments; income and other life insurance; mortgage guarantee insurance; mortgage life insurance; premiums for personal life liability, accident and disability; and other non–health insurance other than homes and vehicles.

market share The market share is the percentage of total household spending on an item that is accounted for by a demographic segment. Market shares are calculated by dividing a demographic segment's total spending on an item by the total spending of all households on the item. Total spending on an item for all households is calculated by multiplying average spending by the total number of households. Total spending on an item for each demographic segment is calculated by multiplying the segment's average spending by the number of households in the segment. Market shares reveal the demographic segments that account for the largest share of spending on a product or service.

millennial generation Americans born between 1977 and 1994.

occupation The occupation in which the reference person received the most earnings during the survey period. The occupational categories follow those of the Census of Population. Categories shown in the tables include the following:

• *self-employed* Includes all occupational categories; the reference person is self-employed in own business, professional practice, or farm.

• *wage and salary earners, managers and professionals* Includes executives, administrators, managers, and professional specialties such as architects, engineers, natural and social scientists, lawyers, teachers, writers, health diagnosis and treatment workers, entertainers, and athletes.

• *wage and salary earners, technical, sales, and clerical workers* Includes technicians and related support workers; sales representatives, sales workers, cashiers, and sales-related occupations; and administrative support, including clerical.

• *retired* People who did not work either full- or part-time during the survey period.

owner See housing tenure.

pensions and Social Security Includes all Social Security contributions paid by employees; employees' contributions to railroad retirement, government retirement and private pensions programs; retirement programs for self-employed.

personal care Includes products for the hair, oral hygiene products, shaving needs, cosmetics, bath products, suntan lotions, hand creams, electric personal care appliances, incontinence products, other personal care products, personal care services such as hair care services (haircuts, bleaching, tinting, coloring, conditioning treatments, permanents, press, and curls), styling and other services for wigs and hairpieces, body massages or slenderizing treatments, facials, manicures, pedicures, shaves, electrolysis.

quarterly spending Quarterly spending data are collected in the interview portion of the Consumer Expenditure Survey. Quarterly spending tables show the percentage of households that purchased an item during an average quarter, and the amount spent during the quarter on the item by purchasers. Not all items are included in the interview portion of the Consumer Expenditure Survey.

reading Includes subscriptions for newspapers, magazines, and books through book clubs; purchase of single-copy newspapers and magazines, books, and encyclopedias and other reference books.

reference person The first member mentioned by the respondent when asked to "Start with the name of the person or one of the persons who owns or rents the home." It is with respect to this person that the relationship of other consumer unit members is determined. Also called the householder or head of household.

region Consumer units are classified according to their address at the time of their participation in the survey. The four major census regions of the United States are the following state groupings:

• *Northeast* Connecticut, Maine, Massachusetts, New Hampshire, New Jersey, New York, Pennsylvania, Rhode Island, and Vermont.

• *Midwest* Illinois, Indiana, Iowa, Kansas, Michigan, Minnesota, Mississippi, Nebraska, North Dakota, Ohio, South Dakota, and Wisconsin.

• *South* Alabama, Arkansas, Delaware, District of Columbia, Florida, Georgia, Kentucky, Louisiana, Maryland, Mississippi, North Carolina, Oklahoma, South Carolina, Tennessee, Texas, Virginia, and West Virginia.

• *West* Alaska, Arizona, California, Colorado, Hawaii, Idaho, Minnesota, Nevada, New Mexico, Oregon, Utah, Washington, and Wyoming.

renter See housing tenure.

shelter Includes the following:

• *owned dwellings* Includes interest on mortgages, property taxes and insurance, refinancing and prepayment charges, ground rent, expenses for property management and security, homeowner's insurance, fire insurance and extended coverage, landscaping expenses for repairs and maintenance contracted out (including periodic maintenance and service contracts), and expenses of materials for owner-performed repairs and maintenance for dwellings used or maintained by the consumer unit, but not dwellings maintained for business or rent.

• *rented dwellings* Includes rent paid for dwellings, rent received as pay, parking fees, maintenance, and other expenses.

• *other lodging* Includes all expenses for vacation homes, school, college, hotels, motels, cottages, trailer camps, and other lodging while out of town.

• *utilities, fuels, and public services* Includes natural gas, electricity, fuel oil, coal, bottled gas, wood, other fuels; residential telephone service, cell phone service, phone cards; water, garbage, trash collection; sewerage maintenance, septic tank cleaning; and other public services.

size of consumer unit The number of people whose usual place of residence at the time of the interview is in the consumer unit.

state and local income taxes Includes state and local income taxes withheld in the survey year to pay for income earned in survey year plus additional taxes paid in the survey year to cover any underpayment or underwithholding of taxes in the year prior to the survey.

tobacco and smoking supplies Includes cigarettes, cigars, snuff, loose smoking tobacco, chewing tobacco, and smoking accessories such as cigarette or cigar holders, pipes, flints, lighters, pipe cleaners, and other smoking products and accessories.

transportation Includes the following:

• *vehicle purchases* (net outlay) Includes the net outlay (purchase price minus trade-in value) on new and used domestic and imported cars and trucks and other vehicles, including motorcycles and private planes.

• *gasoline and motor oil* Includes gasoline, diesel fuel, and motor oil.

• *other vehicle expenses* Includes vehicle finance charges, maintenance and repairs, vehicle insurance, and vehicle rental licenses and other charges.

• *vehicle finance charges* Includes the dollar amount of interest paid for a loan contracted for the purchase of vehicles described above.

• *maintenance and repairs* Includes tires, batteries, tubes, lubrication, filters, coolant, additives, brake and transmission fluids, oil change, brake adjustment and repair, front-end alignment, wheel balancing, steering repair, shock absorber replacement, clutch and transmission repair, electrical system repair, repair to cooling system, drive train repair, drive shaft and rear-end repair, tire repair, vehicle video equipment, other maintenance and services, and auto repair policies.

• *vehicle insurance* Includes the premium paid for insuring cars, trucks, and other vehicles.

• *vehicle rental, licenses, and other charges* Includes leased and rented cars, trucks, motorcycles, and aircraft, inspection fees, state and local registration, drivers' license fees, parking fees, towing charges, tolls on trips, and global positioning services.

• *public transportation* Includes fares for mass transit, buses, trains, airlines, taxis, private school buses, and fares paid on trips for trains, boats, taxis, buses, and trains.

weekly spending Weekly spending data are collected in the diary portion of the Consumer Expenditure Survey. The data show the percentage of households that purchased an item during the average week, and the amount spent per week on the item by purchasers. Not all items are included in the diary portion of the Consumer Expenditure Survey.